WILLIAMS-SONOMA

main dishes
new healthy kitchen

RECIPES

Georgeanne Brennan

GENERAL EDITOR

Chuck Williams

PHOTOGRAPHY

Dan Goldberg & Ben Dearnley

fP
FREE PRESS

NEW YORK • LONDON • TORONTO • SYDNEY

contents

About this book

The books in the New Healthy Kitchen series were created to offer simple and appealing ways to enjoy a diet rich in fruits, vegetables, and grains.

In our modern world, we are fortunate to have a bounty of foods to choose from, but it's easy to make unhealthy choices or to get stuck in a food rut. Since the foods you eat directly affect your overall health and your energy level, incorporating a wide selection of fresh produce and whole grains into your diet and cooking your own meals are two of the best things you can do to eat both healthfully and well.

The recipes in this book are organized in a new way: by the color of the key vegetables or fruits used in the dish. This approach highlights the different nutritional benefits that each color group contributes to your overall health. By thinking about the color of foods, you can be sure to include all the fresh produce you need in your diet. If you consume at least one vegetable or fruit from each color group daily, you can feel confident you are getting the number of servings required for optimum health. Whole grains and legumes have a chapter of their own and, like fresh produce, form a foundation of a wholesome diet.

The New Healthy Kitchen will bring color and creativity into your kitchen, while encouraging you to use a wide variety of fresh produce, legumes, and whole grains and cook them in dishes that preserve their wonderful flavors and essential nutrients.

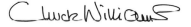

Eating the rainbow

Purple and blue fruits and vegetables contain fiber, vitamins, and phytochemicals that promote heart health; help memory function; lower the risk of some cancers; promote urinary tract health; and boost immunity

Green fruits and vegetables contain fiber, vitamins, and phytochemicals that lower the risk of breast, prostate, lung, and other cancers; promote eye health; help build strong bones and teeth; and boost immunity

White and tan fruits and vegetables contain fiber, vitamins, and phytochemicals that promote heart health; help maintain healthful cholesterol levels; lower the risk of breast, lung, and other cancers; and slow cholesterol absorption

Red fruits and vegetables contain fiber, vitamins, and phytochemicals that promote heart health; help memory function; lower the risk of certain cancers; promote urinary tract health; and boost immunity

Yellow and orange fruits and vegetables contain fiber, vitamins, and phytochemicals that promote heart health; promote eye health; lower the risk of some cancers; and boost immunity

Brown whole grains, legumes, seeds, and nuts include fiber, vitamins, and phytonutrients that lower blood cholesterol levels and reduce the risk of colon and other cancers, diabetes, heart disease, and stroke

Adapted from educational materials of the Produce for Better Health Foundation

The new healthy kitchen

Healthy food is good food, simply cooked to bring out its appealing flavor and beautifully presented to delight the senses. This starts with carefully choosing the best vegetables and fruits, then preparing them with an eye to preserving their inherent colors and textures and their valuable nutrients. The recipes in this cookbook are designed to bring freshness, color, and variety to your table.

The philosophy of the books in the New Healthy Kitchen series is no more complex than this: Eating moderate amounts of a wide range of foods, especially fresh seasonal produce and grains that have not been over-refined and overprocessed, is the key to a healthy diet. Rather than counting calories, fat grams, or carbohydrates, simply focus on keeping your diet constantly varied and rich in fresh vegetables and fruits, whole grains,

and legumes. If consuming these foods is the first priority of your diet each day, you will find that a healthier balance of other foods naturally follows.

Our modern diet is remarkably restricted in the kind of plant foods we eat. With the abundance of all types of food at our disposal, we tend to overindulge in concentrated sources of energy, especially animal fats. We also gravitate toward carbohydrates, which

are excellent sources of quick energy, but unfortunately our most common forms of carbohydrates, such as refined flours, are stripped of the wholesome nutrients found in whole grains.

And while taking a daily multivitamin is not a bad idea, popping supplement pills isn't a good solution to a lack of vitamins and minerals in the diet. Your body can make better use of these compounds when it

extracts them in their natural state from food. Eating a variety of plant foods is the best way of getting what you need, and in a form in which your body is designed to use it.

Some of the benefits of eating fruits and vegetables come from the vitamins, minerals, and fiber they contain, while other benefits come from a newly discovered class of nutrients called phytonutrients, or phyto-chemicals. These plant compounds work in a number of ways to protect our bodies and fight disease. In many cases, phytochemicals are the elements in fruits and vegetables that give them their distinctive colors and flavors. So the dazzling hues of vegetables and fruits, from bright red tomatoes to dark green spinach to deep purple eggplant, give clues to the particular phytonutrients each contains.

Eating a rainbow of produce will give you the broadest array of health benefits from all these various nutrients.

In addition to fruits and vegetables, a good portion of the food you eat daily should come from another group of plant foods: grains and legumes. These foods are rich in fiber, protein, complex carbohydrates, and minerals, plus phytochemicals of their own. To get the most benefit from grains, they should be eaten whole, or minimally pro-cessed and as close to their natural state as possible.

To guide your meal planning, the chapters in this cookbook are organized by the five prominent color groups of vegetables and fruits: purple and blue; green; white and tan; yellow and orange; and red. A sixth chapter

focuses on "brown" foods like whole grains, legumes, nuts, and seeds. Paying attention to the colors of healthy foods when you prepare meals will bring a cornucopia of ingredients, some of them new or over-looked, into your daily fare.

Each colorful chapter begins with a chart showing which fruits and vegetables are at their peak of ripeness each season. The Brown chapter chart shows which grains, legumes, nuts, and seeds might figure in a hearty main dish.

The recipes of the New Healthy Kitchen are simple and straightforward, designed for real-life cooks who haven't much time to spare, but want to use the time they do have to cook and eat creatively, colorfully, and—above all—*well*.

Fruits & vegetables

Fruits and vegetables are the cornerstone of a healthy diet. They are also some of the most beautiful and delicious foods on the planet—a boon to both the eye and the palate, with tastes and textures that range from bitter greens to sweet cherries. The recipes in *Main Dishes* will inspire you to add new fruits and vegetables to your meals and reap the benefits of their vitamins, minerals, and phytochemicals.

In the early years of the twentieth century, one after another, the various vitamins and minerals we now know are essential to maintaining good health and fighting disease were discovered. We are now entering into a similarly exciting era of discovery, as we learn about the roles that phytochemicals play in our bodies.

These protective compounds, which are believed to number in the thousands, work alone and in combination with one another and with nutrients. They work in different ways. For example, some phytochemicals act as antioxidants, protecting the body by neutralizing unstable oxygen molecules (known as free radicals) that damage cells and promote disease. Regularly eating plant foods rich in antioxidants can reduce the incidence of various cancers, heart disease, impaired vision, and other health problems.

Fruits and vegetables from each of the color groups provide us with different combination of phytonutrients, each playing a unique role in fighting disease and promoting health and well-being.

By eating fruit and vegetables at their peak of ripeness, you will not only be pleasing your palate, but you will also be giving your body the benefit of all the healthy nutrients that these foods contain.

Grains & legumes

Grains and legumes are traditional starchy accompaniments for meats and vegetables. The term "breaking bread" has long been synonymous with enjoying a meal, and legumes like chickpeas and kidney beans have sustained people in the Middle East and Latin America for generations. But wholesome carbohydrates—the complex kind—have been a recent victim of the latest diet craze.

Like vegetables and fruits, grains and legumes—which are the seeds of plants—contain a wealth of nutrients. They are rich in vitamins and minerals, fiber, and phytochemicals as well. In our modern diet, however, grains are usually refined, in the form of white wheat flour and white rice, with the fiber-rich hull and the nutrient-rich germ removed. The quantity of whole grains and legumes we consume overall has sharply dropped over the past several decades.

In the New Healthy Kitchen, recipes emphasizing grains, legumes, nuts, and seeds are grouped in a chapter called Brown. These foods come in a variety of colors, but thinking of them as brown will help remind you that

they should be as close to their natural state as possible. Whole grains have more flavor than refined grains. This, combined with their nutritional value, makes them equal companions to meats and vegetables, rather than merely bland backdrops.

The recipes in this book encourage you to try a range of grains, such as barley, quinoa, and bulgur, in their whole forms. The classic bulgur salad tabbouleh becomes a hearty meal with the addition of scallops (page 114), while barley can be sautéed with mushrooms to make a savory side (page 118) to accompany a recipe from another chapter in this book. Brown rice cooks up chewy and delicious and can be substituted for white

rice as an accompaniment to a stir-fry with beef and black beans (page 114).

Legumes, the seeds of plants with pods that split open when dried, include peas, beans, lentils, and peanuts. They contain fiber, complex carbohydrates, and some iron, plus enough protein that they can substitute for meat, fish, or poultry, allowing you to enjoy the occasional meatless meal.

Other seeds, such as flaxseed, sesame seeds, and nuts, can add flavor, texture, color, and excellent nutrition to recipes. Cashews, for instance, enhance a chicken and brown rice salad (page 120), and sesame seeds make a tasty garnish for a stir-fry (page 23).

Other ingredients

The colorful eating philosophy of the New Healthy Kitchen makes fresh vegetables and fruits and whole grains and legumes the foundation of a good diet. But other foods, like meat and dairy products have places the New Healthy Kitchen. Even fats, in moderation, are essential to good health and add flavor, interest, and texture, while various seasonings and condiments add zest to your meals.

Consuming too much fat is never advisable, but you do require a small amount of fat daily to help your body and particularly your brain function at its best. Olive, canola, and grape seed oils bring out the flavors of produce and satisfy our instinctive craving for unctuous fat. These three oils are particularly valuable due to their high content of monounsaturated fat, which is better for you than other kinds of fats. Monounsaturated fats

help lower the level of bad cholesterol and boost the level of good cholesterol, and they can routinely be used to cook and dress foods.

Other oils can be added to foods in small amounts, as you would a condiment, to contribute their unique flavors to salads and vegetable dishes. These include nut and seed oils, such as walnut and toasted sesame, and extra-virgin olive oils. Only a teaspoon of intensely earthy truffle oil, for

example, is necessary for drizzling over the top of Celery Root and Potato Potpie (page 64). A few tablespoons of orange-infused olive oil add a citrusy undertone to a purée of root vegetables (page 79).

Nothing can replace butter for its sweet flavor and luxurious and satisfying texture. Only a little is needed as the finishing touch to a sauce or soup. In this book, a small amount of butter is often combined with olive oil for browning meat such as beef medallions (page 23), cooking frittatas (pages 27 and 102), and sautéing shallots and other aromatic vegetables.

Strongly flavored high-fat meats likewise serve as flavor enhancers. Bacon, prosciutto, and pancetta play a role in the New Healthy Kitchen series, contributing a satisfying dimension to otherwise meatless dishes. Pancetta makes an appealing addition to a chowder with yellow corn and salmon (page 79). A few strips of bacon are crumbled into small pieces as an option for garnishing Brussels sprouts and scallops (page 50).

Many cheeses are assertively flavored yet fairly low in fat, such as fresh goat cheese and feta cheese and grating cheeses like Parmesan, Gruyère, and pecorino. They make good toppings for gratins and are also classic garnishes for pasta. Both goat cheese and Parmesan cheese grace a butternut squash pizza (page 76). In all cases, cheeses provide extra calcium in a form more easily digestible than milk.

Dairy products like light sour cream, heavy cream, and crème fraîche are nice finishing touches to soups and sauces when used with restraint. If you are particularly concerned with lowering the fat in your diet, you can mix half of the quantity called for in a recipe with an equal amount of plain yogurt, or replace them entirely with yogurt.

Spices, like fresh herbs, add both color and flavor to foods. Their impact on the palate far exceeds the very small amounts used in a recipe. Ground or whole spices lend their distinctive notes to many recipes in this book: star anise in a stew with carrots and beef (page 82) and cumin and paprika in a salad of chickpeas (garbanzo beans) and corn (page 124). To maximize the characteristic flavor of a spice, it is best to purchase whole spices and grind them with a mortar and pestle, a spice grinder, or an electric coffee grinder kept just for this purpose. Purchase spices in small amounts and store in airtight jars for up to a year in order to preserve flavor.

Vinegars serve as instant flavor boosters. They range from delicate sherry vinegars to rich aged balsamics. Assertive vinegars such as aged red wine are best used in small quantities. Two vinegars are featured in a recipe for game hens (page 95): raspberry vinegar is part of a seasoning mixture brushed on the hens before roasting, and balsamic gives a slight tang to the sauce.

Creating the healthy meal

Committing to eating a healthful diet based on vegetables, fruits, legumes, and whole grains may require you to make some changes in your day-to-day life. You might need to modify your shopping habits, visiting the market once a week or more for fresh produce, or to reduce portions if you've grown accustomed to supersizing. But the rewards truly outweigh any inconveniences.

To find the best fresh produce, seek out just-harvested, locally grown vegetables and fruits in season at a specialty produce market or a natural foods store. Or, better yet, make a visit to the farmers' market or farm stand part of your weekend recreation. Although organic produce costs more than conventional, pesticide-free fruits and

vegetables that are locally grown and picked at the peak of ripeness also taste better and have their nutrients still intact.

If your ingredients are high in quality, only the simplest techniques are needed to cook them. This is the approach you'll find through-out the recipes in *Main Dishes*. Vegetables are steamed, stir-fried, sautéed, grilled, or

roasted just long enough to transform their textures or bring out their flavors. Similarly, fruits are briefly poached or sautéed. Many recipes in this book, such as salads, salsas, and relishes, use vegetables and fruits raw.

Raw vegetables and fruits are also used to garnish finished dishes in *Main Dishes*. Arranged attractively on the plate, whole or sliced vegetables and fruits contribute visual interest and nutritional variety. Fresh herbs, whether chopped or left as sprigs, can be scattered on top of a finished dish. Seeds and chopped nuts make excellent garnishes.

Creating visual appeal extends to the presentation of food. A main dish with colorful produce can be served on pure white dishes or on contrasting, brightly colored ones. When you plan meals using recipes in the various color groups, you will also want to consider the Fresh Ideas in each chapter. This special feature includes very simple ways to use an item in each color group. Some Fresh Ideas, such as the onions stuffed with sausage and egg (page 63), the baked acorn squash topped with dried fruit and nuts (page 81),

and the radicchio and dried cranberry salad (page 100), serve as light main dishes in themselves. You can also combine two Fresh Ideas to make a main course. Or, serve braised mixed greens (page 44), blue potato chips (page 28), or shallots braised in wine (page 62) as side dishes. Simple ideas like sautéed purple figs (page 29), blackberry pan sauce (page 29), and broiled tomatoes (page 101) are excellent accompaniments to meat or fish that has been simply grilled, roasted, or sautéed.

Because the Fresh Ideas allow you adjust the amounts of ingredients to suit the number of servings you need, you'll want to keep the moderate portions in mind. As a visual cue, a reasonable portion of cooked, boneless meat,

poultry, or seafood is about the size of a deck of playing cards. Similarly, a serving of raw leafy vegetables is the size of half of a baseball. Imagine a tennis ball when you are preparing a serving of sliced fruit.

The recipes in the New Healthy Kitchen are deliberately simple and streamlined. Preparation and cooking times are listed at the beginning of the recipe to help you fit them into your daily routine. Many main dishes can be prepared in a half hour or a little more, making them perfect for a delightful midweek supper.

The recipes in *Main Dishes* are designed to inspire you to create your own healthy kitchen, exploring all the wonderful variety of fresh and wholesome foods nature provides.

eggplants prunes blackberries

PURPLE AND BLUE FRUITS AND VEGETABLES PROMOTE

purple carrots black currants

MEMORY FUNCTION • HELP PROMOTE URINARY TRACT

lavender blue potatoes purple

HEALTH • BOOST THE IMMUNE SYSTEM • HELP PROMOTE

cabbage raisins black grapes

HEALTHY AGING • OFFER ANTIOXIDANTS FOR HEALING

purple figs blue plums purple

AND PROTECTION • HELP REDUCE THE RISK OF SOME

bell peppers purple asparagus

CANCERS • PURPLE AND BLUE FRUITS AND VEGETABLES

Purple & blue

These are not the first colors that come to mind when you think of food. Purple and blue vegetables and fruits, some of the most unusual produce in the market, are rarities in nature. But rare things are generally valuable, and this is certainly true of the produce in this color group. A number of vegetables usually found in other colors have purple varieties, among them asparagus, carrots, and potatoes.

Many berry varieties crowd the ranks of the blue category: not only blueberries and blackberries, but also olallieberries, marionberries, and currants. Berries may seem more of a treat than a health food, but recent nutritional research indicates that they are more beneficial than once believed due to their high antioxidant content.

In this chapter, you'll find many appealing ways to prepare blue and purple vegetables and fruits. A blueberry sauce offers an intriguing complement to medallions of beef (page 23). Wilted purple cabbage forms a bed for sautéed apples and a modest amount of sausage (page 33) in a streamlined version of Alsatian choucroute.

Be sure to take advantage of fresh figs when they are in season in late summer and early autumn, even for savory main-course dishes. Figs are delicious eaten out of hand, but cooking the figs makes them plump and even softer, intensifying their rich flavor and making them a luscious counterpoint to quail (page 27).

SPRING	SUMMER	AUTUMN	WINTER
purple asparagus	purple bell peppers	purple-tipped Belgian endive	purple-tipped Belgian endive
purple-tipped Belgian endive	blackberries	purple bell peppers	purple cabbage
blueberries	blueberries	blueberries	purple carrots
purple cabbage	fresh black currants	purple cabbage	dried currants
purple carrots	eggplant	purple carrots	blue, purple, and black grapes
dried currants	purple figs	dried currants	purple potatoes
blue, purple, and black grapes	lavender	eggplant	prunes
prunes	blue, purple, and black plums	purple figs	raisins
raisins		blue, purple, and black grapes	
		blue, purple, and black plums	
		blue potatoes	
		prunes	
		raisins	

beef medallions
with blueberry sauce

⅓ cup (2 oz/60 g) all-purpose (plain) flour

1 lb (500 g) beef tenderloin, sliced crosswise ½ inch (12 mm) thick

1 Tbsp butter

2 tsp olive oil

3 Tbsp minced shallots

3 Tbsp brandy

1½ cups (6 oz/185 g) fresh or frozen blueberries

½ cup (4 fl oz/125 ml) low-sodium chicken broth

Whisk flour, 1 tsp salt, and 1 tsp pepper together in a bowl. Spread on a plate. Dredge meat in flour to coat, shaking off excess.

Melt butter with oil in a frying pan over medium-high heat. Sauté meat in batches until lightly browned, about 2 minutes per side. Using a wire skimmer or tongs, remove to a plate and keep warm in a low (150°F/65°C) oven. Add shallots and cook for 30 seconds. Add brandy and stir to scrape up browned bits.

Reduce heat to medium and stir in blueberries. Add broth, raise heat to medium-high, and cook until reduced to about ⅓ cup (3 fl oz/80 ml), 4–5 minutes. To serve, place meat on a warmed platter and spoon sauce on top.

To prepare: 15 minutes

To cook: 15 minutes

4 servings

purple asparagus
& chicken stir-fry

15–20 purple or green asparagus spears, trimmed

2 Tbsp canola oil

2 Tbsp minced fresh ginger

2 cloves garlic, minced

2 Tbsp finely chopped green (spring) onion, white part only

1 lb (500 g) skinless, boneless chicken breasts, cubed

1 Tbsp sherry vinegar

2 tsp light soy sauce

25–30 fresh basil leaves

1 tsp sesame seeds

Cut asparagus on the bias into pieces 1 inch (2.5 cm) long. Set aside.

Heat oil in a wok over high heat until almost smoking. Add ginger, garlic, and green onion and stir-fry until fragrant, about 30 seconds. Reduce heat to medium-high, add chicken, and stir-fry until opaque, 3–4 minutes. Using a wire skimmer, remove chicken to a bowl. Add asparagus to wok and stir-fry until tender-crisp, about 3 minutes. Add vinegar and soy sauce and stir to scrape up browned bits. Return chicken to wok, add basil, and stir-fry until basil is wilted, 15–20 seconds.

Using a slotted spoon, remove stir-fry to a serving bowl, sprinkle with sesame seeds, and serve.

To prepare: 15 minutes

To cook: 10 minutes

4 servings

grilled eggplant sandwiches with aioli

¼ cup (2 fl oz/60 ml) olive oil

1 globe eggplant (aubergine),
cut lengthwise into slices
½ inch (12 mm) thick

Aioli

2 cloves garlic, halved

1 whole egg plus 1 egg yolk, at room
temperature

½ cup (4 fl oz/250 ml) *each*
extra-virgin olive oil and canola oil,
mixed together

Focaccia squares, split horizontally, or
8–10 slices country-style bread, each
sliced ½ inch (12 mm) thick

Lettuce leaves for serving

Build a hot wood or charcoal fire in a grill, or preheat a gas grill to 400°F (200°C). Rub hot grill rack with 1 tsp of olive oil.

Coat eggplant slices on both sides with a little olive oil and sprinkle with salt and pepper. Grill until golden, 6–7 minutes. Turn and grill on second side until golden, about 4 minutes. Remove and set aside.

For Aioli: Combine garlic and ½ tsp salt in a mortar or small bowl and crush to a paste with a pestle or back of a spoon. Transfer paste to a food processor, add egg and egg yolk, and pulse 2 or 3 times. With machine running, add oil drop by drop at first, then in a fine stream until mixture is thick and emulsified, about 2–4 minutes. Remove to a bowl and stir in ½ tsp pepper and salt to taste.

Spread bread slices with aioli. Place grilled eggplant and a lettuce leaf on half of slices. Top with another bread slice and serve at once. Cover leftover aioli and store in refrigerator for up to 12 hours.

To prepare: 25 minutes

To cook: 25 minutes

4 or 5 servings

quail with roasted fresh figs

8 quail

1 tsp sweet paprika

1 Tbsp olive oil

12 purple figs

2 tsp minced fresh rosemary, plus 4 sprigs for optional garnish

Preheat oven to 450°F (230°C). Rub quail inside and out with paprika, 1 tsp salt, and 1 tsp pepper. Tie their legs together with kitchen twine.

Heat oil in an ovenproof frying pan over medium-high heat. Add quail in batches as needed and sear on all sides until lightly browned, about 5 minutes. Add figs and stir to coat with pan juices. Sprinkle figs and quail with minced rosemary. Place in oven and roast until figs are plump and breast meat of quail is still slightly pink, 7–10 minutes.

To serve, place 2 quail and 3 figs on each warmed plate and drizzle with pan juices. Garnish with a rosemary sprig, if using.

To prepare: 20 minutes

To cook: 20 minutes

4 servings

roasted purple pepper frittata

2 purple, red, or yellow bell peppers (capsicums)

6 eggs

2 Tbsp whole or low-fat milk

¼ cup (1 oz/30 g) grated Parmesan cheese

1 Tbsp butter

1 Tbsp olive oil

¼ onion, chopped

1 clove garlic, minced

2 Tbsp minced fresh oregano or marjoram

1 tsp minced fresh thyme

Preheat a broiler (grill). Slide bell peppers under broiler (grill) about 4 inches (10 cm) from heat source and broil, turning occasionally, until blackened, about 5 minutes per side. Transfer to a paper bag and let sweat for 5 minutes. Peel, seed, and chop peppers. Set aside.

Beat eggs, milk, cheese, ¾ tsp salt, and ½ tsp pepper together in a bowl until just blended. Melt butter with oil in a 10-inch (25-cm) frying pan over medium-high heat. Add onion and sauté until translucent, 2–3 minutes. Add garlic and sauté until fragrant. Add peppers, spread out evenly, and pour egg mixture over them. Reduce heat to low and cook until eggs are set around edges, 3–4 minutes. Using a spatula, lift edges of eggs and tilt pan to let uncooked eggs run under. Cook until top is nearly set, 4–5 minutes.

Invert a plate on top of pan and, holding plate and pan firmly together with a pot holder, flip them to turn frittata out onto plate. Sprinkle half of the herbs into pan and slide frittata back into pan, cooked side up. Cook for 1–2 minutes, then invert a plate over pan and flip again. Sprinkle with remaining herbs. Serve hot or at room temperature, cut into wedges.

To prepare: 30 minutes

To cook: 25 minutes

4 servings

blue potato chips

Cut blue potatoes into paper-thin slices. Heat 1½ inches (4 cm) canola oil in a deep cast-iron frying pan over medium heat until oil reaches 375°F (190°C). Fry potato slices. Drain on paper towels, sprinkle with sea salt, and serve at once.

blueberry wild rice

Cook wild rice or brown rice until tender, according to package directions. Drain and sauté in olive oil, along with blueberries, chopped onion, walnuts, celery, and prunes until rice is golden brown and flavors have melded.

sautéed purple figs

Cut figs in half. Heat olive oil in a pan over medium heat. Sauté finely chopped shallot. Add figs and sauté for 2 minutes, until shiny and warmed through. Add balsamic vinegar to the pan and cook to reduce to a light glaze for figs.

blackberry pan sauce

After meat or chicken has been sautéed in a pan, add balsamic vinegar and chicken broth to pan over medium heat and stir to scrape up browned bits. Add blackberries and minced rosemary and cook until sauce is slightly thickened.

prune, raisin & lamb stew with almonds

2 Tbsp olive oil

1½ lb (750 g) cubed lamb stew meat

¼ cup (1 oz/30 g) finely chopped onion

3 cloves garlic, minced

½ tsp ground cumin

1 tsp chili powder

1 Tbsp all-purpose (plain) flour

2 Tbsp brandy

1½ cups (12 fl oz/375 ml) low-sodium chicken broth

3 poblano chiles, seeded and thinly sliced lengthwise

¼ cup (1 oz/30 g) almonds, coarsely chopped

12 pitted prunes, coarsely chopped

¼ cup (1½ oz/45 g) raisins

Heat olive oil over medium-high heat in a Dutch oven or heavy stockpot. Working in batches, add lamb and brown on all sides, about 4 minutes. Remove each batch to a bowl. Add onion and garlic and return lamb to pan along with any juices. Stir well, reduce heat to medium, and sprinkle with cumin, chili powder, flour, ½ tsp salt, and ½ tsp pepper. Stir until lamb is well coated, about 1 minute. Add brandy and stir to scrape up browned bits. Stir in ¼ cup (2 fl oz/60 ml) water and chicken broth. Bring to a boil, reduce heat to low, cover, and simmer gently, until stew is slightly reduced and flavors are blended, 35–40 minutes. Add chiles and continue to simmer, covered, until lamb is tender, 15–20 minutes more.

Meanwhile, preheat oven to 350°F (180°C). Spread almonds on a baking sheet and toast until fragrant, about 10 minutes.

Stir half the prunes and raisins into stew. Raise heat to high and stir until liquid is thickened, 3–5 minutes. Remove from heat and stir in remaining raisins and prunes. Serve at once, garnished with toasted almonds.

To prepare: 30 minutes

To cook: 70 minutes

4 servings

purple cabbage, apples & bratwurst

1½ Tbsp olive oil

¼ cup (1 oz/30 g) chopped onion

½ head purple cabbage, cored and thinly sliced lengthwise

1 cup (8 fl oz/250 ml) low-sodium chicken broth

1 Tbsp butter

3 Golden Delicious apples, cored and thinly sliced

4 bratwursts

1 Tbsp cider vinegar or lemon juice

Heat oil in a frying pan over medium-high heat. Add onion and sauté until translucent, 2–3 minutes. Add cabbage, 1 tsp salt, and ½ tsp pepper and sauté until cabbage begins to wilt, about 5 minutes. Reduce heat to medium, cover, and cook for 5 minutes more. Add chicken broth, reduce heat to low, cover, and cook until most of the liquid is absorbed and cabbage is tender, about 15 minutes.

Meanwhile, melt butter in a frying pan over medium-high heat. Add apples and sauté until golden on both sides, about 5 minutes total. Using a slotted spoon, transfer to a plate and keep warm. Reduce heat to medium, add bratwursts, and cook, turning occasionally, until golden on all sides, about 10 minutes. Stir vinegar into cabbage. Serve bratwursts on top of cabbage, sliced if desired, surrounded by apples.

To prepare: 20 minutes

To cook: 30 minutes

4 servings

chicken breasts with purple grape sauce

4 bone-in, skin-on chicken breast halves

2 tsp minced fresh rosemary

1 Tbsp olive oil

½ cup (2½ oz/75 g) finely chopped red onion

2 cloves garlic, minced

1 cup (8 fl oz/250 ml) low-sodium chicken broth

½ cup (4 fl oz/125 ml) ruby port

3 cups (18 oz/560 g) purple seedless grapes, halved

Rub chicken with rosemary, 1 tsp salt, and 1 tsp pepper. In a sauté pan, heat olive oil over medium-high heat. Add chicken, skin side down, and cook until golden, 3–4 minutes. Turn, add onion and garlic to pan, and cook, stirring onion and garlic, for 3–4 minutes. Add ¾ cup (6 fl oz/180 ml) of broth and stir to scrape up browned bits. Reduce heat to low, cover, and cook until chicken is opaque throughout, 35–40 minutes.

Remove chicken to a platter and keep warm in a low (150°F/65°C) oven. Pour off clear fat from pan, leaving pan juices. Add port, raise heat to high, and cook until reduced to about ½ cup (4 fl oz/125 ml). Stir in all but ½ cup (3 oz/90 g) grapes and cook until they begin to soften, about 3 minutes. Add remaining ¼ cup (2 fl oz/70 ml) broth. To serve, pour pan sauce over chicken and garnish with remaining grapes.

To prepare: 20 minutes

To cook: 50 minutes

4 servings

avocados cucumbers spinach

GREEN FRUITS AND VEGETABLES BOOST THE IMMUNE

watercress arugula asparagus

SYSTEM • PROMOTE EYE HEALTH • HELP BUILD STRONG

kale broccoli snow peas leeks

BONES • BUILD STRONG TEETH • OFFER ANTIOXIDANTS

lettuce zucchini green beans

FOR HEALING AND PROTECTION • REDUCE THE RISK OF

endive brussels sprouts limes

CERTAIN CANCERS • GREEN FRUITS AND VEGETABLES

green tea kiwifruits artichokes

BOOST THE IMMUNE SYSTEM • PROMOTE EYE HEALTH

Green

Associated with growing things, green is the color that first comes to mind when the subject is vegetables. Green-colored fruits share the same qualities of pureness and freshness. Green produce comes in many forms—leafy greens, silken avocados, crisp green apples and pears, and the nutrition-packed cruciferous family, which includes broccoli, Brussels sprouts, bok choy, and cabbage.

Eating green vegetables doesn't have to be a chore, as may be the case if you are accustomed to old-fashioned boiled vegetables. Blanching, steaming, and sautéing, quick ways to prepare vegetables, preserve their natural textures and flavors and leave more nutrients intact. If you have always encountered overcooked Brussels sprouts, the recipe in this chapter—which sautés them until golden and partners them with tender scallops—will change your opinion of this oft-maligned vegetable.

Curry (page 40) and risotto (page 39) are great vehicles for green vegetables such as the snow peas (mangetouts) and spinach featured here. Fresh green parsley, rich in antioxidants, appears in a relish (page 43) used to dress perfectly cooked tuna.

Avocados are fruits traditionally paired with savory foods, making an appearance here in pita pockets with chicken (page 43). The green grapes and pears in the duck salad on page 46 give you two of the day's servings of fruit in a single main dish.

SPRING	SUMMER	AUTUMN	WINTER
artichokes	arugula	green apples	green apples
asparagus	avocados (Hass)	artichokes	avocados (Fuerte)
green bell peppers	green chiles	bok choy	bok choy
endive	cucumbers	broccoli	broccoli
green beans	green beans	broccoli rabe	broccoli rabe
kiwifruits	herbs	Brussels sprouts	Brussels sprouts
Persian and Key limes	Persian and Key limes	green cabbage	green cabbage
lettuce	green-fleshed melons	endive	celery
green pears	okra	green grapes	endive
English peas	sugar snap peas	kale	kale
snow peas	spinach	leeks	leeks
sugar snap peas	zucchini	green pears	snow peas
spinach		Swiss chard	spinach
watercress		watercress	watercress

shrimp, baby spinach & basil risotto

½ lb (500 g) medium shrimp (prawns), shelled and deveined

2 cups (16 fl oz/500 ml) low-sodium chicken broth

2 Tbsp butter

2 Tbsp olive oil

2 Tbsp minced shallot

1½ cups (10½ oz/330 g) Arborio rice

4 cups (4 oz/125 g) baby spinach leaves, cut into fine shreds

1 cup (1 oz/30 g) finely sliced fresh basil

¼ cup (1 oz/30 g) grated Parmesan cheese (optional)

Reserve 8 shrimp and coarsely chop the rest. Combine broth and 3 cups (24 fl oz/750 ml) water in a saucepan and bring to a boil over medium-high heat. Reduce heat to low. Add whole shrimp and cook until bright pink, 2–3 minutes. Remove with a slotted spoon and set aside.

Melt 1 Tbsp butter with olive oil in a large, heavy saucepan over medium-high heat. Add shallot and sauté until softened, about 1 minute. Add rice and sauté until opaque, about 3 minutes. Add ¾ cup (6 fl oz/180 ml) broth mixture, reduce heat to medium and cook, stirring, until most of liquid is absorbed. Stir in chopped shrimp. Continue to add ¾ cup broth at intervals until almost all liquid is used and rice is al dente, about 20 minutes. Add a Tbsp or two broth to rice and stir in spinach and basil, remaining butter, salt to taste, and cheese, if using. Serve at once, garnished with whole shrimp.

To prepare: 25 minutes

To cook: 25 minutes

4 servings

artichokes stuffed with orzo & feta salad

4 large artichokes

Salad

1 cup (7 oz/220 g) orzo pasta

1 small tomato, finely chopped

2 tsp lemon juice

2–3 Tbsp extra-virgin olive oil

½ cup (3 oz/90 g) crumbled feta cheese

6–8 large basil leaves, finely chopped

¼ cup (⅓ oz/10 g) minced fresh parsley

1 Tbsp red wine vinegar

Cut off thorny upper third of each artichoke and trim stem to within ½ inch (12 mm) of base. Place artichokes upside down in a covered steamer over simmering water and cook until fork-tender, about 50 minutes, adding water as needed. Using a slotted spoon, remove to a plate and set upside down.

For Salad: Meanwhile, cook orzo in a large pot of salted boiling water until al dente, 10–12 minutes. Drain and spread on a platter. Stir in tomato, lemon juice, 1 Tbsp oil, ½ tsp salt, and ½ tsp pepper. Let cool. Stir in feta, basil, parsley, and vinegar, plus oil to taste.

Using a teaspoon, scoop out choke in center of each artichoke, scraping out any fuzzy or purple bits. Gently spread leaves apart. Fill with some orzo salad. Tuck a teaspoonful of salad into base of some leaves. Serve at room temperature.

To prepare: 25 minutes

To cook: 50 minutes

4 servings

snow peas & chicken green curry

1½ Tbsp canola oil

1 tsp Thai green curry paste

3 skinless, boneless chicken thighs or 1 skinless, boneless chicken breast, thickly sliced crosswise

½ tsp Asian fish sauce

1 cup (8 fl oz/250 ml) light coconut milk

3 Tbsp low-sodium chicken broth

½ long green chile, seeded and minced

½ lb (250 g) snow peas (mangetouts), trimmed

½ lb (250 g) button mushrooms, thinly sliced

Steamed rice for serving

Heat oil in a large frying pan over medium-high heat. Add curry paste and stir-fry for about 45 seconds. Add chicken and stir-fry until opaque, 3–4 minutes. Add fish sauce and a little coconut milk and stir to scrape up browned bits. Add remaining coconut milk, broth, and chile and cook, stirring, until liquid is reduced to ⅔ cup (5 fl oz/160 ml), 6–7 minutes. Add snow peas and mushrooms and cook for 1–2 minutes more.

Serve hot, over steamed rice.

Note: Green curry paste is available at Asian markets and well-stocked grocery stores.

To prepare: 10 minutes

To cook: 15 minutes

4 servings

orecchiette with spicy broccoli rabe

1 bunch broccoli rabe, tough stem ends removed, cut into 1½-inch (4-cm) pieces

3 Tbsp olive oil

2 large cloves garlic, minced

1 tin (2 oz/60 g) oil-packed anchovies, plus their oil

¼ tsp red pepper flakes

10 oz (315 g) orecchiette pasta

¼ cup (1 oz/30 g) grated Parmesan cheese

Add broccoli rabe to a large pot of salted boiling water and cook for 4 minutes. Drain and set aside. Heat oil over medium heat in a frying pan. Add garlic and sauté just until pale gold. Add anchovies and their oil, mashing with back of a spoon. Add broccoli rabe, red pepper flakes, and ¼ tsp black pepper and cook, stirring frequently, until greens are very tender, about 5 minutes. Remove from heat and keep warm.

Cook orecchiette in a large pot of salted boiling water until al dente, 12–15 minutes. Drain and put in a bowl. Add broccoli rabe and sauce. Toss to coat pasta. Sprinkle with cheese and serve at once.

To prepare: 20 minutes

To cook: 25 minutes

4 servings

pan-seared tuna
with parsley relish

Relish

2 cloves garlic, coarsely chopped

¼ cup (2 fl oz/60 ml) extra-virgin olive oil

1 cup (1½ oz/45 g) minced fresh parsley

1 tsp lemon juice

2 tsp minced shallot

4 ahi tuna steaks, each 5 oz (155 g) and ½ inch (12 mm) thick

1 Tbsp olive oil

For Relish: Put garlic, oil, and ¼ tsp salt in a blender or food processor and purée. Add parsley and lemon juice and process to a coarse relish. Stir in shallot. Taste and adjust seasoning. Set aside.

Heat a heavy frying pan over medium-high heat for 2 minutes. Brush tuna on both sides with oil and season with 1½ tsp salt and 1½ tsp pepper. Add tuna to pan and sear until bottom of each steak is opaque and beginning to brown, about 2 minutes. Turn and sear second side for medium-rare. Top with some of the parsley relish and serve the remainder at table.

Note: Serve with Shiitakes Sautéed with Garlic (page 63).

To prepare: 20 minutes

To cook: 10 minutes

4 servings

chicken pockets
with avocado salsa

¾ lb (12 oz/375 g) skinless, boneless chicken breasts

2 tsp canola oil

2 Tbsp lime juice

Salsa

2 avocados, peeled and pitted

¼ cup (1½ oz/45 g) seedless green grapes

½ cup (2½ oz/75 g) cashews, chopped

1 serrano chile, seeded and minced

1 Tbsp lime juice

2 pita breads, toasted and cut in half

2 Tbsp minced fresh cilantro (fresh coriander) or parsley

Sprinkle chicken with a scant ½ tsp salt and a scant ½ tsp pepper. Heat oil in a frying pan over medium-high heat. Add chicken and cook until lightly golden, 1–2 minutes per side. Add ¼ cup (2 fl oz/60 ml) water and lime juice. Cover, reduce heat to low, and cook just until chicken is opaque throughout, about 2 minutes. Remove chicken and set aside.

For Salsa: Cut avocados into ½ inch (12-mm) dice. Slice grapes in half. Gently stir avocados, cashews, grapes, chile, lime juice, ¼ tsp salt, and ¼ tsp pepper together in a bowl. Taste and adjust seasoning.

Coarsely chop chicken. Divide among pita halves, placing it into pockets. Fill each pocket with avocado salsa and garnish with cilantro.

To prepare: 30 minutes

To cook: 5 minutes

4 servings

grilled baby artichokes

Coat baby artichokes with olive oil, then season with salt, pepper, and minced fresh thyme. Grill over medium-hot coals, turning occasionally, until fork-tender, about 15 minutes. Serve warm, with lemon juice for dipping.

braised mixed greens

Mix together escarole (Batavian endive), kale, chard, and spinach. Put in a sauté pan with a little water and cook until limp, 3–5 minutes. Drain and sauté in olive oil with salt, pepper, and minced garlic. Cover and cook briefly until soft.

savory broccoli sauté

Sauté broccoli florets in olive oil over medium heat until softened, letting them sizzle and brown. Add chopped green olives, capers, lemon zest, dried red pepper flakes, and garlic. Sauté until broccoli is golden and flavors melded.

roast brussels sprouts

Peel away outer layer of leaves and cut Brussels sprouts in half. Toss with olive oil, salt, pepper, and minced fresh oregano or thyme. Put in a baking dish and roast, turning occasionally, until golden and fork-tender.

cod braised
with bok choy

2 Tbsp soy sauce, plus more for
serving

2 Tbsp dry white wine

½ clove garlic, minced

1 tsp minced fresh ginger

1 head bok choy, trimmed and
coarsely chopped

4 cod or other firm fish fillets,
4 oz (125 g) each

Stir 2 Tbsp soy sauce, wine, garlic, and ginger together in a small bowl.
Set aside.

Immerse bok choy in a bowl of water. Lift from water to a large sauté
pan. Place over medium-high heat, add ¼ cup (2 fl oz/60 ml) water,
cover, and reduce heat to low. Cook until tender, 4–5 minutes.

Pour off liquid, return to low heat, and stir in soy sauce mixture. Place
fish fillets on top of bok choy, cover, and cook until fish is opaque throughout, about 4 minutes. Serve accompanied with soy sauce.

To prepare: 15 minutes

To cook: 10 minutes

4 servings

green grape, pear
& duck salad

1 duck breast half, about 1 lb (500 g)

½ tsp ground coriander

2 Tbsp minced shallot

2 Tbsp balsamic vinegar

2 cups (12 oz/375 g) seedless green
grapes, some halved

2 bunches watercress, stemmed
(about 4 cups/4 oz/125 g)

2 green pears, such as Comice or
Seckel, cored and thinly sliced

Remove skin and fat from duck by pulling fatty layer back and cutting it
from meat with a small knife. Set breast aside. Place fatty layer, skin side
down, in a frying pan over medium heat. Cook, turning occasionally, until
about ¼ cup (2 fl oz/60 ml) fat is rendered, about 10 minutes. Discard
the skin. Measure out 2 Tbsp fat and set aside. Discard the rest or save
for another use.

Raise heat to high. Season duck breast on both sides with 1 tsp salt,
½ tsp pepper, and coriander. Sear until browned, about 3 minutes. Add
shallot, turn duck, and cook on other side for 3 minutes. Reduce heat
to medium and cook until duck is rosy only in the center, 1–2 minutes
more. Transfer to a cutting board and tent with foil. Raise heat to high,
add ½ cup (4 fl oz/125 ml) water, vinegar, and whole grapes to pan, and
stir to scrape up browned bits. Simmer until liquid is reduced to ¼ cup
(2 fl oz/60 ml), about 2 minutes. Slice duck on bias into thin slices. Pour
any collected juices into pan.

Arrange watercress on a platter and top with alternating slices of pear
and duck. Pour grape sauce over, scatter with grape halves, and serve.

To prepare: 30 minutes

To cook: 20 minutes

4 servings

pork cutlets with sautéed kale

2 Tbsp olive oil

2 Tbsp chopped shallot

1 large bunch kale, stemmed and coarsely chopped

½ cup (4 fl oz/125 ml) low-sodium chicken broth

4 pork cutlets, each about ½ inch (12 mm) thick

Heat 1 Tbsp of oil in a large frying pan over medium heat. Add shallot and sauté until translucent, 2–3 minutes. Stir in kale, broth, ½ tsp salt, and ½ tsp pepper. Reduce heat to low, cover, and cook until kale is fork-tender, about 15 minutes.

Meanwhile, rub cutlets on both sides with ½ tsp salt and ½ tsp pepper. Heat remaining 1 Tbsp olive oil in a large, ovenproof frying pan over medium-high heat. Add cutlets and cook until browned, about 2 minutes per side. Reduce heat to medium, cover, and cook until cutlets are opaque throughout, about 4 minutes more. To serve, divide kale among 4 warmed plates and top with cutlets.

To prepare: 15 minutes

To cook: 15 minutes

4 servings

halibut in parchment with zucchini & mint

1½ Tbsp butter

4 halibut fillets, each 5 oz (155 g)

2 Tbsp minced shallot

2 green zucchini (courgettes), shredded

¼ cup (⅓ oz/10 g) minced fresh mint

4 thin lemon slices

Preheat oven to 375°F (190°C). Cut 4 sheets of parchment (baking) paper into rectangles 14 x 20 inches (35 x 50 cm). Fold each in half lengthwise. Cut a large half-heart shape and unfold to make a heart. Using half the butter, butter one side of each paper heart. Set a fillet on the buttered side of each heart. Sprinkle each fillet with one-fourth of shallot, zucchini, and mint, plus ¼ tsp salt and ¼ tsp pepper. Dot with remaining butter and top with a lemon slice. Fold paper over fish and crimp edges to seal.

Place on a baking sheet and bake until paper crisps and turns golden, 15 minutes. To serve, place each packet on a dinner plate for guests to unwrap at table.

To prepare: 15 minutes

To cook: 15 minutes

4 servings

scallops with brussels sprouts & bacon

12 Brussels sprouts, trimmed and quartered lengthwise

4 strips bacon (optional; see Note)

Scallops

12 sea scallops

¼ cup (1 oz/30 g) cornstarch (cornflour)

2 tsp butter

2 tsp olive oil

2 Tbsp lemon juice

2 Tbsp dry white wine

Lemon wedges and extra-virgin olive oil for serving (optional)

Cook Brussels sprouts in a large saucepan of salted water until barely tender. Drain and rinse under cold water to stop cooking.

Meanwhile, put bacon (if using) in a frying pan over medium heat. Cook, turning occasionally, until crisp. Drain on paper towels. Pour off all but 2 tsp rendered bacon fat.

Return frying pan to medium-high heat. Add sprouts and sauté until edges are golden, about 5 minutes. Season with 1 tsp salt and 1 tsp pepper. Remove from heat and cover to keep warm.

For Scallops: Pat scallops dry with paper towels. Mix cornstarch on a plate with ½ tsp salt and ½ tsp pepper. Roll scallops in cornstarch mixture to coat lightly. Melt butter with olive oil in a frying pan over medium-high heat. Add scallops and sear for 3 minutes. Turn and sear second side for 1 minute. Add lemon juice, wine, and 2 Tbsp water and stir to scrape up any browned bits. Cover, reduce heat to low, and cook until scallops are just opaque throughout, 2–3 minutes.

Divide Brussels sprouts among 4 bowls. Top each serving with 3 scallops and drizzle with pan juices. Crumble bacon, if used, and sprinkle over sprouts; or drizzle with lemon juice and olive oil. Serve hot.

Note: If omitting bacon, replace bacon fat with 1 tsp each butter and olive oil for sautéing Brussels sprouts.

To prepare: 25 minutes

To cook: 15 minutes

4 servings

cauliflower shallots mushrooms

WHITE AND TAN FRUITS AND VEGETABLES CONTAIN

dates turnips bananas tan figs

ANTIOXIDANTS FOR HEALING AND PROTECTION • HELP

tan pears parsnips white corn

MAINTAIN A HEALTHY CHOLESTEROL LEVEL • PROMOTE

potatoes jerusalem artichokes

HEART HEALTH • BOOST THE IMMUNE SYSTEM • SLOW

ginger kohlrabi white peaches

CHOLESTEROL ABSORPTION • WHITE AND TAN FRUITS

garlic white nectarines jicama

AND VEGETABLES OFFER ANTIOXIDANTS FOR HEALING

White & tan

This group of fruits and vegetables is not the flashiest. Its appeal is more understated than that of its jewel-toned relatives. But the subdued colors of these vegetables and fruits do not mean that they lack nutrient value. Nor are they deficient in flavor, for white and tan produce ranges widely, from earthy mushrooms to aromatic ginger to silken white nectarines.

One of the important foods in this chapter is the allium family: onions, garlic, shallots, and leeks. Their place in many recipes may seem minor, but the health benefits they offer suggest they should play a leading role, as they do in a stir-fry with a generous amount of onions (page 67) and a hearty stew made with aromatic leeks (page 67).

Many nourishing root vegetables are found in the white and tan category, potatoes and parsnips being two common ones. Among the less familiar choices are knobbly brown celery root (celeriac), jicamas, and Jerusalem artichokes (also known as sunchokes) used here in a warming quick-simmered soup with potatoes and chicken (page 61).

White cauliflower, a member of the nutrient-rich cruciferous family, is a versatile vegetable that stars here in a gratin (page 61) and in a quick-and-easy sauté seasoned with cumin (page 68). Meaty, filling, and a great source of fiber and B vitimins, mushrooms make an ideal meatless main course, as in the rustic tart on page 57.

SPRING	SUMMER	AUTUMN	WINTER
bananas	bananas	bananas	cauliflower
cauliflower	white corn	cauliflower	dates
dates	dates	dates	garlic
garlic	tan figs	tan figs	ginger
ginger	garlic	Jerusalem artichokes	Jerusalem artichokes
jicama	ginger	jicama	jicama
mushrooms	kohlrabi	kohlrabi	dried mushrooms
onions	mushrooms	mushrooms	onions
parsnips	white nectarines	onions	parsnips
tan pears	onions	parsnips	tan pears
potatoes	white peaches	tan pears	potatoes
shallots	tan pears	potatoes	shallots
turnips	potatoes	shallots	turnips
	shallots	turnips	

mushroom galettes

Pastry

1¼ cups (6½ oz/200 g) all-purpose (plain) flour

½ tsp salt

½ cup (4 oz/125 g) cold butter, cut into small pieces

2–3 Tbsp ice water

⅓ cup (2½ oz/75 g) ricotta cheese

Mushrooms

1½ Tbsp butter

1½ Tbsp olive oil

¼ cup (1 oz/30 g) minced shallot

2½ lb (1.25 kg) mixed mushrooms, such as oyster, chanterelle, cremini, and black trumpet, sliced or coarsely chopped

2 tsp minced garlic

2 Tbsp brandy

2 Tbsp minced fresh parsley for garnish

For Pastry: Combine flour and salt in a food processor. Add butter and pulse until mixture resembles small peas. With machine running, gradually add ice water until dough comes together. Gather dough into a ball and divide into 4 smaller balls. Enclose each ball in plastic wrap and flatten into disks. Place in freezer for 30 minutes, or refrigerate overnight.

Preheat oven to 375°F (190°C). On a lightly floured surface, roll out each disk into a round ¼ inch (6 mm) thick. Lay pastry rounds on a baking sheet and bake until lightly golden, 12–15 minutes. Do not overbake. Place pan on a wire rack. Spread each warm round with some ricotta.

For Mushrooms: Melt butter with oil in a frying pan over medium-high heat. Add shallot and sauté until translucent, about 1 minute. Add mushrooms and garlic and sauté until mushrooms are soft, about 3 minutes. Add brandy and stir to scrape up browned bits. Cook until most liquid has evaporated, about 1 minute more.

To serve, place a galette on each of 4 warmed plates and top with mushrooms. Sprinkle with parsley.

To prepare: 20 minutes, plus 30 minutes to chill

To cook: 15 minutes

4 servings

grilled chicken with white peach salsa

1½ lb (750 g) skinless, boneless chicken breasts

1 Tbsp olive oil

½ tsp chili powder or paprika

1 tsp minced fresh thyme

4 white peaches, peeled (optional), pitted, and coarsely chopped

2 Tbsp lime juice

3 Tbsp finely chopped red onion

Put chicken in a bowl. Add oil, chili powder, thyme, ½ tsp salt, and ½ tsp pepper. Turn chicken to coat.

Build a hot wood or charcoal fire in a grill, or preheat a gas grill to 400°F (200°C). Grill chicken until golden brown, about 2 minutes per side. Cover grill and cook just until chicken is opaque throughout, 2–3 minutes. Remove to a platter and tent with foil.

Stir peaches, lime juice, and onion together in a bowl. Spoon salsa on top of chicken or serve alongside.

To prepare: 30 minutes

To cook: 7 minutes

4 servings

grilled flank steak with white corn relish

4 ears white corn

4 Tbsp (2 fl oz/60 ml) olive oil

2 red bell peppers (capsicums)

2 Tbsp minced fresh oregano or marjoram

1 flank steak, about 1½ lb (750 g)

1 tsp minced fresh rosemary

Build a hot wood or charcoal fire in a grill, or preheat a gas grill to 400°F (200°C). Pull back corn husks but leave them attached; remove corn silk and brush corn with some oil. Sprinkle with ¾ tsp salt and ¾ tsp pepper. Replace husks.

Grill bell peppers, turning occasionally, until blackened, about 5 minutes. Remove to a paper bag and let sweat for 5 minutes. Meanwhile, grill corn for 10 minutes, turning frequently. Pull back husks and grill kernels, turning, until browned, 2–3 minutes. Remove from grill and let cool.

Cut kernels from cobs. Peel, seed, and dice peppers. Stir corn kernels, peppers, oregano, 2 Tbsp olive oil, ½ tsp salt, and ½ tsp pepper together in a bowl.

Brush flank steak on both sides with remaining oil. Season with rosemary, ¼ tsp salt, and ¼ tsp pepper. Sear until still slightly pink only in center, 2–3 minutes per side. Remove and let rest for 5 minutes. Slice against grain on bias. Serve with salsa on top or alongside.

To prepare: 25 minutes

To cook: 25 minutes

4 servings

chicken & jerusalem artichoke soup

2 Tbsp olive oil

¼ cup (1 oz/30 g) chopped yellow onion

2 skinless, boneless chicken breast halves, each 6 oz (185 g)

2 cloves garlic, minced

½ lb (250 g) Jerusalem artichokes (sunchokes), peeled and thinly sliced

3 carrots, sliced

4 small potatoes, halved

1 tsp minced fresh sage

2 stalks chard, very thinly sliced crosswise

¼ cup (2 fl oz/60 ml) lime juice

Heat oil in a large saucepan over medium-high heat. Add onion and sauté until translucent, 2–3 minutes. Cut each chicken half breast into 4 or 5 pieces. Add chicken to pan and cook, turning, until surface is opaque, about 2 minutes. Add garlic, Jerusalem artichokes, carrots, and potatoes. Stir once or twice, add 2 cups (16 fl oz/500 ml) water, ½ 1 tsp salt, ¼ tsp pepper, sage, and chard.

Reduce heat to low, cover, and simmer until potatoes are tender and chicken is opaque throughout, 25–30 minutes. Add lime juice. Taste and adjust seasoning with salt. Serve hot in deep bowls.

To prepare: 35 minutes

To cook: 35 minutes

4 servings

cauliflower gratin

1 head cauliflower, cut into large florets

1 Tbsp olive oil

2 oz (60 g) pancetta, chopped

1 yellow onion, thinly sliced

4 oz (125 g) Muenster cheese, thinly sliced

Preheat oven to 350°F (180°C). Butter a baking dish just large enough to hold cauliflower in a single layer.

Cook cauliflower in a covered steamer over simmering water until fork-tender, 10–15 minutes. Remove to prepared dish.

Heat oil in a frying pan over medium heat. Add pancetta and onion and sauté until pancetta is crisp and onion is golden, about 15 minutes. Spoon over cauliflower and sprinkle with ½ tsp pepper. Top with cheese to cover evenly. Bake until edges are bubbling and cheese is beginning to brown, about 20 minutes. Serve hot.

To prepare: 15 minutes

To cook: 50 minutes

4 servings

mashed parsnips with parsley

Peel and cut parsnips into chunks; cook in salted boiling water until tender. Drain and return to pan. Add a little milk, salt, pepper, butter, and minced fresh parsley. Mash with potato masher, taste and adjust seasoning, and serve hot.

shallots braised in wine

Peel shallots, halve if large, and sauté in olive oil until lightly browned, adding a sprinkle of sugar as they color. Add a little white wine, salt and pepper to taste, and some chicken broth. Cover and braise until very tender and nearly caramelized.

shiitakes sautéed with garlic

Stem and quarter the shiitake mushrooms. Sprinkle the mushrooms with minced garlic, salt, pepper, and minced fresh parsley. Sauté in olive oil until they are just beginning to get crisp on the outside.

roasted stuffed onions

Hollow out white onions, leaving a shell about ½ inch (12 mm) thick. Fill onions with a mixture of Italian sausage, egg, and fresh bread crumbs. Place in a baking dish with ½ inch (12 mm) water and bake at 350°F (180°C) for about 1 hour.

celery root & potato potpie

Pastry

1¼ cups (6½ oz/200 g) all-purpose (plain) flour

½ tsp salt

½ cup (4 oz/125 g) cold butter, cut into small pieces

2–3 Tbsp ice water

1 large or 2 medium celery roots (celeriacs), peeled and cut into ½-inch (12-mm) dice

1 lb (500 g) potatoes, peeled and cut into ½-inch (12-mm) dice

2 Tbsp butter

½ cup (2 oz/60 g) chopped yellow onion

4 stalks celery, chopped

2 tsp all-purpose (plain) flour

3 cups (24 fl oz/750 ml) low-sodium chicken broth

2 Tbsp minced fresh parsley

1 tsp black truffle oil

For Pastry: Combine flour and salt in a food processor. Add butter and pulse until mixture resembles small peas. With machine running, gradually add ice water until dough comes together. Gather dough into a ball. Enclose in plastic wrap and flatten into a disk. Place in freezer for 30 minutes, or refrigerate overnight.

Combine celery roots and potatoes in a saucepan. Add water to cover and ½ tsp salt. Bring to a boil over medium-high heat, reduce heat to medium, and cook until vegetables are fork-tender, 7–10 minutes. Drain.

Melt butter in a frying pan over medium-high heat. Add onion and celery and sauté until onion is translucent, 4–5 minutes. Sprinkle with flour and ½ tsp salt and stir well. Gradually stir in broth and cook until reduced to about 2 cups (16 fl oz/500 ml). Stir in parsley. Remove from heat and set aside.

Preheat oven to 400°F (200°C). On a lightly floured surface, roll out pastry disk into a round about ⅛ inch (6 mm) thick and trim to fit a 6- to 8-cup (180- to 250-ml) casserole dish.

Put potatoes and celery root in casserole. Pour reduced broth mixture on top. Drizzle with truffle oil. Cover with pastry, pinching edges to seal. Cut 2 or 3 slits in top. Bake until crust is golden brown and edges are bubbling, 15–20 minutes.

Remove from oven and let stand for 10 minutes before serving. Slice and spoon into warmed bowls to serve.

To prepare: 50 minutes, plus 30 minutes to chill

To cook: 45 minutes

4–6 servings

beef, ginger & white onion stir-fry

¾ lb (375 g) beef sirloin

6 small white or 2 yellow onions

1 small egg, lightly beaten

1 Tbsp cornstarch (cornflour)

1 cup (8 fl oz/250 ml) canola oil

2 Tbsp soy sauce

2 tsp sugar

½ tsp Asian sesame oil

½ tsp rice wine vinegar

One 2-inch (5-cm) piece fresh ginger, peeled and thinly sliced crosswise

Steamed brown rice or cooked soba noodles for serving

Fresh parsley for garnish

Thinly slice beef against the grain and set aside.

Cut onions lengthwise into quarters, then cut in half crosswise. If using larger onions, separate into pieces. Set aside. In a bowl, stir together beef and egg. Stir in cornstarch and 1 tsp oil. Let stand for 30 minutes.

In a small bowl, mix together soy sauce, sugar, sesame oil, vinegar, and 2 Tbsp water. Set aside. Heat remaining oil in a wok over medium-high heat until almost smoking. Using a slotted spoon, transfer beef to hot oil. Cook until color changes, then remove to a platter using slotted spoon. Add onions and ginger and stir-fry until onion is translucent then remove to the platter with the beef. Pour off all but 1 Tbsp oil and add soy sauce mixture; simmer for 2–3 minutes to thicken. Stir in beef, onion, and ginger to coat. Serve hot over rice or noodles, garnished with parsley.

To prepare: 15 minutes

To cook: 10 minutes

4 servings

leek & new potato stew with bockwurst

1 Tbsp butter

4 leeks, white and pale green parts, cut lengthwise into thin strips

4 cups (32 fl oz/1 l) low-sodium chicken broth

1¼ lb (20 oz/625 g) new white potatoes, peeled or unpeeled, cut into ½-inch (12-mm) pieces

3 bockwursts, cut crosswise into slices ½ inch (12 mm) thick

1 tsp olive oil

Melt butter in a large saucepan over medium-high heat. Add leeks and sauté until translucent, 3–4 minutes. Add broth and 1 cup (8 fl oz/ 250 ml) water and bring to a rapid simmer. Add potatoes, reduce heat to low, and simmer until potatoes begin to break apart, about 20 minutes.

Meanwhile, cut each bockwurst slice into quarters. Heat oil in a nonstick frying pan over medium heat. Add sausage and cook, turning, until lightly browned, about 5 minutes. Add to saucepan and simmer for 3–4 minutes to blend flavors. Season to taste with salt and pepper.

Serve hot, ladled into warmed bowls.

To prepare: 15 minutes

To cook: 35 minutes

4 servings

cauliflower & potato sauté with cumin

1 small head cauliflower

3 white potatoes, peeled and cut into slices

1 Tbsp butter

2 Tbsp olive oil

1½ tsp ground cumin

1 tsp paprika

Cook cauliflower head whole in a covered steamer over boiling water until fork-tender, about 20 minutes. Remove and let cool.

Put potatoes in a saucepan with water to cover. Bring to a boil over medium-high heat. Reduce heat to medium and cook until fork-tender, 15–20 minutes. Drain and let cool.

Cut cauliflower into 2-inch (5-cm) pieces, leaving as many florets intact as possible.

Melt butter with olive oil in a frying pan over medium-high heat. Add potatoes and cauliflower, sprinkle with cumin, paprika, and 1 tsp salt, and sauté, turning gently, until potatoes are golden brown and cauliflower is lightly browned, about 5 minutes. Serve hot.

Note: Serve with Couscous with Peas & Mint (page 123).

To prepare: 5 minutes

To cook: 40 minutes

4 servings

pork & parsnip braise

1 Tbsp olive oil

3 lb (1.5 kg) country-style pork ribs, cut into 2-inch (5-cm) pieces

¼ cup (2 fl oz/60 ml) dry sherry

1½ cup (12 fl oz/375 ml) low-sodium beef broth

3 parsnips, peeled and cut into pieces ½ inch (12 mm) wide and 2 inches (5 cm) long

Chopped fresh parsley for garnish

Preheat oven to 375°F (190°C).

Heat oil in a large ovenproof sauté pan with a lid over medium-high heat. Season pork with 1 tsp salt and ½ tsp pepper. Working in batches, sear pork until lightly browned, about 2 minutes per side. Remove and set aside.

Pour sherry and a little broth into the pan over medium-high heat and stir to scrape up browned bits. Remove from heat. Return pork to pan and add parsnips. Pour in remaining broth, cover, and braise in oven until meat and parsnips are fork-tender, about 1 hour. Serve hot, garnished with parsley.

To prepare: 20 minutes

To cook: 70 minutes

4 servings

grapefruit papayas pineapples

YELLOW AND ORANGE FRUITS AND VEGETABLES HELP

apricots yellow pears pumpkins

PROMOTE HEART HEALTH • HELP REDUCE THE RISK OF

persimmons peaches kumquats

CERTAIN CANCERS • PROMOTE EYE HEALTH • CONTAIN

rutabagas golden beets carrots

ANTIOXIDANTS FOR HEALING AND PROTECTION • BOOST

yellow apples golden kiwifruits

THE IMMUNE SYSTEM • YELLOW AND ORANGE FRUITS

lemons navel oranges mangoes

AND VEGETABLES OFFER ANTIOXIDANTS FOR HEALING

Yellow & orange

Sweet potatoes, pumpkins, apricots, and oranges—the vegetables and fruits in this color group are eye-catching and appealing. The list of produce here is extensive, too, especially since it includes produce commonly found in other colors, such as beets and raspberries, that have yellow and orange forms. This color offers a range of tastes and textures in addition to significant health benefits.

Among the more creative uses for orange and yellow produce offered in this chapter is a crisp-crusted pizza topped with chunks of butternut squash and dotted with goat cheese (page 76). Or, try combining chopped fresh apricots with minced chile and herbs in a salsa that is the perfect accompaniment for lamb chops (page 75).

A number of root vegetables make the list of each season's best selections, below. Both yellow-fleshed potatoes and bright orange yams are cooked with turkey thighs, making a dish ideal for autumn and winter when the two vegetables are in season (page 85). An ample quantity of carrots, one of the most common orange vegetables, stars in

an uncommon dish—a beef stew spiced with star anise (page 82).

Citrus fruits are an interesting addition to main dishes. Oranges and tangerines mingle with avocado in a refreshing crab salad (page 86). Each bite offers a flavor and texture sensation, along with a welcome measure of vitamin C.

SPRING	SUMMER	AUTUMN	WINTER
carrots	apricots	yellow apples	yellow apples
grapefruit	yellow bell peppers	dried apricots	dried apricots
golden kiwifruits	corn	golden beets	golden beets
kumquats	mangoes	yellow bell peppers	carrots
lemons	orange-fleshed melon	lemons	grapefruit
mangoes	nectarines	navel and Mandarin oranges	kumquats
navel & Mandarin oranges	Valencia oranges	yellow pears	lemons
papayas	papayas	persimmons	navel and Mandarin oranges
yellow-fleshed potatoes	peaches	yellow-fleshed potatoes	yellow pears
orange-fleshed winter squash	pineapples	pumpkins	yellow-fleshed potatoes
sweet potatoes	golden raspberries	rutabagas	pumpkins
	yellow summer squash	orange-fleshed winter squash	rutabagas
	yellow tomatoes	sweet potatoes	orange-fleshed winter squash
			sweet potatoes

honey-glazed lamb chops
with apricot salsa

8 apricots, pitted and chopped

1 serrano chile, seeded and minced

1 tsp minced shallot

¼ cup (⅓ oz/10 g) chopped fresh cilantro (fresh coriander)

2 Tbsp lime juice

1 tsp plus 2 Tbsp lavender honey

1 rack of lamb, (1–1¼ lb/500–625 oz), trimmed and frenched

¼ tsp each dried thyme and dried rosemary, crushed

1¼ tsp ground dried lavender blossoms (optional)

1 Tbsp olive oil

Stir apricots, chile, shallot, cilantro, lime juice, and 1 tsp honey together in a small bowl to make salsa. Set aside.

Preheat oven to 475°F (245°C). Rub lamb with thyme, rosemary, 1 tsp of lavender (if using), 1 tsp salt, and 1 tsp pepper. Heat oil in a heavy, ovenproof frying pan over medium-high heat. Sear lamb, fat side down, for 1–2 minutes. Sear each end for 1 minute. Sear bone side for about 2 minutes. Leave rack bone side down. Put lamb in oven and roast for 15–20 minutes for medium-rare (an instant-read thermometer inserted in thickest part away from bone should read 130°F/54°C). During final 5 minutes of roasting, baste lamb with 2 Tbsp honey.

Remove from oven, tent with foil, and let rest for 5 minutes. Sprinkle with remaining lavender (if using) and carve between ribs into chops. Serve at once, accompanied with the salsa.

To prepare: 20 minutes

To cook: 30 minutes

4 servings

arctic char with yellow beets
& horseradish sauce

4 or 5 yellow beets, stems trimmed to ½ inch (12 mm)

2 Tbsp olive oil

¼ cup (2 oz/60 g) prepared horseradish

2 Tbsp light sour cream

4 arctic char or trout fillets, 4–5 oz (125–155 g) each

1 tsp freshly squeezed lemon juice, plus 4 lemon wedges for garnish

2 Tbsp minced fresh parsley

Preheat oven to 350°F (180°C). Coat beets with 1 Tbsp of oil. Put in a shallow baking dish just large enough to hold them in a single layer. Roast beets until tender, about 1 hour. Remove from oven and let cool. Trim, peel, and dice beets. Set aside.

Raise oven temperature to 450°F (230°C). Stir horseradish, sour cream, and ¼ tsp salt together in a small bowl. Taste and adjust seasoning. Using half of remaining oil, grease a baking dish just large enough to hold fillets in a single layer. Place fillets in prepared baking dish, drizzle with remaining oil and lemon juice, and sprinkle with ½ tsp salt and ½ tsp pepper. Bake until fish is opaque throughout, about 10 minutes.

To serve, make a bed of diced beets on each warmed plate. Top with a fillet and drizzle some horseradish sauce over beets and fish. Sprinkle with parsley and garnish with a lemon wedge.

To prepare: 25 minutes

To cook: 70 minutes

4 servings

butternut squash pizza

Dough

1 envelope (2½ tsp) active dry yeast

1 cup (8 fl oz/250 ml) warm (105°–115°F/40°–46°C) water

1 tsp sugar

2½–3 cups (12½–15 oz/390–470 g) all-purpose (plain) flour

3 Tbsp extra-virgin olive oil

1 tsp salt

2 Tbsp cornmeal

Topping

1½ lb (750 g) butternut squash

4 Tbsp (2 fl oz/60 ml) olive oil

1 tsp minced fresh thyme

3–4 oz (90–125 g) soft goat cheese

¼ cup (1 oz/30 g) grated Parmesan cheese

½ cup (½ oz/15 g) baby arugula (rocket) leaves (optional)

For Dough: Dissolve yeast in the warm water in a small bowl. Add sugar and let stand for 5 minutes. Put 2½ cups (12½ oz/390 g) flour in a food processor and add yeast mixture, 2 Tbsp of oil, and salt. Process until a ball forms. Add remaining flour a little at a time, processing until a glossy, not sticky, dough ball forms.

Turn dough out onto a lightly floured surface and knead until elastic, about 7 minutes. Let dough rest for 5 minutes. Place in a bowl, drizzle with remaining oil, turn to coat, and cover with a damp towel. Let rise in a warm place until doubled, 1½–2 hours.

Divide dough in half. Flatten each half and roll each half into a disk about 12 inches (30 cm) in diameter. Sprinkle 2 baking sheets with cornmeal and lay a disk on each.

For Topping: Preheat oven to 350°F (180°C). Halve and seed squash, then cut into slices 2 inches (5 cm) thick. Put squash in a bowl and add 2 Tbsp of oil, 1 tsp salt, 1 tsp pepper, and thyme. Turn to coat well. Place on a baking sheet and bake until fork-tender, about 1¼ hours. Let cool to touch. Cut flesh away from skin. Cut flesh into bite-sized pieces.

Raise oven temperature to 500°F (260°C). Drizzle each dough disk with 2 tsp of oil. Dot with pieces of squash and goat cheese. Sprinkle with Parmesan. Bake until crust is browned and goat cheese is slightly melted, 12–15 minutes. Remove and drizzle with remaining olive oil and garnish with arugula, if using.

To prepare: 45 minutes, plus 2 hours to rise

To cook: 1½ hours

Two 12–inch (30-cm) pizzas; 4 servings

salmon & yellow corn chowder with pancetta

2 oz (60 g) pancetta, cut into 1-inch (2.5-cm) pieces

1–2 tsp butter, if needed

½ cup (2½ oz/75 g) finely chopped yellow onion

2 stalks celery, finely chopped

4¼ cups (36 fl oz/1.1 l) milk

Kernels cut from 5 ears yellow corn, cobs reserved

1 russet potato, peeled and diced

1 salmon fillet, about 10 oz (315 g), skin and pin bones removed, cut into ½-inch (12-mm) pieces

1 Tbsp minced fresh chives

Cook pancetta in a large saucepan over medium heat until it renders some of its fat, about 5 minutes. (If there is not enough fat in pan to sauté, add 1 tsp butter.) Add onion and celery and sauté until translucent, 2–3 minutes. Add milk, reserved corn cobs, potato, 1 tsp salt, and ½ tsp pepper. Cover, reduce heat to medium-low, and simmer for 15 minutes.

Remove and discard cobs. Stir in corn kernels, raise heat to medium, and cook for 5 minutes. Scoop out 1 cup (8 fl oz/250 ml) soup and coarsely purée in a blender, then return to pan. Add salmon and cook just until barely opaque, 2–3 minutes. Taste and adjust seasoning.

To serve, ladle into warmed bowls and garnish with fresh chives.

To prepare: 40 minutes

To cook: 30 minutes

4 or 5 servings

broiled chicken with carrot & potato purée

4 skin-on, bone-in chicken breast halves, about ⅔ lb (330 g) each

2 tsp fresh thyme leaves

4 Yukon Gold potatoes, peeled and quartered

2 carrots, peeled and cut into 2-inch (5-cm) lengths

3 Tbsp extra-virgin olive oil blended with 1 Tbsp grated orange zest

1 Tbsp minced fresh parsley

Preheat a broiler (grill). Season chicken breasts with 1 tsp salt, 1 tsp pepper, and thyme. Place on a baking sheet and slide under broiler 8 inches (20 cm) from heat source. Broil (grill) chicken, turning once, until opaque throughout, about 45 minutes. (If you cannot cook chicken this far from heat source, bake at 350°F/180°C until opaque throughout, 35–40 minutes.)

Meanwhile, put potatoes and carrots in a large saucepan with water to cover by 2 inches (5 cm). Add 1 Tbsp salt and bring to a boil over high heat. Reduce heat to medium and cook until vegetables are fork-tender, about 20 minutes. Drain and return to saucepan. Coarsely mash with a potato masher. Add oil, 1½ tsp salt, and ½ tsp pepper. Remove to a serving dish and sprinkle with parsley. Serve with broiled chicken.

To prepare: 20 minutes

To cook: 45 minutes

4 servings

roasted yellow beets

Trim greens from small yellow beets, leaving a little stem and tails intact. Wrap in foil and roast at 400°F (200°C) until tender, about 1 hour (depending on size). Peel and quarter, drizzle with extra-virgin olive oil, season with salt and pepper, and top with goat cheese and minced chives.

mango lassi

This refreshing Indian drink helps offset the fiery effect of chile, so serve it with or after a spicy meal. It can be made either salty or sweet according to your preference. Purée fresh mango flesh with plain yogurt, lemon juice, and ice cubes. Add sugar or salt to taste.

baked acorn squash

Halve an acorn squash lengthwise, seed, then cut crosswise into 1-inch (2.5-cm) slices and fill each slice with a mixture of chopped prunes and walnuts mashed with butter. Sprinkle with a little cinnamon, salt, and pepper. Bake at 350°F (180°C) until squash is fork-tender.

simple orange salad

Cut navel oranges into crosswise slices ¼ inch (6 mm) thick and cut away the colored rind and white pith. Place the orange slices on a bed of arugula (rocket) or other salad greens and dress lightly with vinaigrette and a sprinkle of toasted pine nuts.

grilled trout with golden squash kabobs

8 sunburst squash or yellow zucchini (courgettes), cut into chunks ½ inch (12 mm) thick

2 tsp minced fresh thyme

2 Tbsp olive oil

2 slices thick bacon, cut into ½-inch (12-mm) pieces (optional)

4–8 trout fillets, 3–6 oz (90–185 g) each

Toss squash in a bowl together with thyme, 1 Tbsp of oil, and ½ tsp pepper. Let marinate for about 45 minutes, tossing occasionally.

Soak 4 long or 8 short wooden skewers in water for 30 minutes. Build a hot wood or charcoal fire in a grill, or preheat a gas grill to 400°F (200°C). Alternately thread squash and bacon, if using, onto skewers. Grill until squash is lightly browned and bacon begins to crisp, 3–4 minutes per side. Remove to a platter. Brush fillets on both sides with remaining oil and sprinkle with ½ tsp salt. Place fillets, skin side down, on grill. Cover and cook until fish is opaque throughout, 4–5 minutes. Remove to a platter. To serve, arrange 1 or 2 fillets on each plate and top with a kabob or two. Or, remove squash and bacon (if using) from skewers, mound on plate, and top with fish.

To prepare: 20 minutes, plus 45 minutes to marinate

To cook: 15 minutes

4 servings

beef & carrot stew with star anise

2 Tbsp olive oil

1 cup (4 oz/125 g) chopped yellow onion

3 cloves garlic, minced

1½ lb (750 g) boneless chuck or other stewing beef, cut into 2-inch (5-cm) cubes

2 cups (16 fl oz/500 ml) dry red wine

2 lb (1 kg) carrots, peeled and cut into 1-inch (2.5-cm) lengths

1 Tbsp minced fresh thyme

1 bay leaf

2 star anise pods

1 cup (8 fl oz/250 ml) water or low-sodium beef broth, if needed

1 Tbsp minced fresh parsley

Heat oil in a large Dutch oven or heavy stockpot over medium-high heat. Add onion and sauté until translucent, 5 minutes. Add garlic and sauté for 1 minute. Remove onion and garlic to a large bowl. Pat meat dry with paper towels. Working in batches, brown meat on all sides, 5–7 minutes. Remove to bowl with onion and garlic.

Add half of red wine to pan and stir to scrape up browned bits. Return meat, onion, garlic, and collected juices to pan along with remaining red wine, carrots, thyme, bay leaf, star anise, 1 tsp salt, and ½ tsp pepper. Reduce heat to low, cover, and gently simmer, stirring every 15 minutes or so, for 1 hour. Taste for seasoning and continue cooking, stirring every 15 minutes until meat is fork-tender, 1½–2 hours more. Add water or broth if liquid evaporates to less than ½ inch (12 mm) deep. Serve in warmed bowls, garnished with parsley.

To prepare: 30 minutes

To cook: 3¼ hours

4 servings

roast pork loin with rutabagas & apples

1 Tbsp Dijon mustard

1½ tsp packed brown sugar or honey

¼ tsp ground ginger

¾ lb (12 oz/375 g) rutabagas, peeled and cut into 1-inch (2.5-cm) cubes

2 Granny Smith apples, cored and cut into slices 1 inch (2.5 cm) thick

1 Tbsp olive oil

1½ tsp minced fresh rosemary

2 lb (1 kg) boneless pork loin

1 bay leaf

Preheat oven to 450°F (230°C). Stir mustard, sugar, and ginger together in a small bowl. Set aside.

Put rutabagas and apples in a bowl and add olive oil, ¾ tsp salt, ¾ tsp pepper, and half of rosemary. Turn to coat well. Rub pork loin on all sides with ¾ tsp salt, ¾ tsp pepper, and remaining rosemary.

Put pork, rutabagas, and apples in a roasting pan just large enough to hold them snugly in a single layer. Tuck in bay leaf. Roast for 15 minutes. Reduce heat to 350°F (180°C). Roast for 20 minutes, then gently turn rutabagas and apples. Spread mustard mixture on meat and continue to roast until meat is firm to touch and an instant-read thermometer inserted in center reads 145°F (63°C) for medium-well, 15–20 minutes.

Remove from oven, tent with aluminum foil, and let rest for 10 minutes. Carve into slices ½ inch (12 mm) thick. Serve hot with rutabagas, apples, and pan juices.

To prepare: 30 minutes

To cook: 40 minutes

4 servings

---

slow-braised turkey thighs, potatoes & yams

¼ cup (2 fl oz/ 60 ml) olive oil

1½ lb (750 g) skinless, boneless turkey thighs

4 Yukon Gold potatoes, peeled and cubed

2 yams (orange-fleshed sweet potatoes), peeled and cubed

1½ tsp minced fresh rosemary

1–2 cups (8–16 fl oz/250–500 ml) low-sodium chicken broth

2 Tbsp minced fresh parsley

Preheat oven to 350°F (180°C). Heat oil in a Dutch oven or heavy stockpot over medium-high heat. Add turkey and brown, 3–4 minutes per side. Remove from heat, add potatoes and yams to pan, and turn to coat in oil. Sprinkle with half of rosemary, 1 tsp salt, and 1 tsp pepper. Add enough broth to reach ½ inch (12 mm) up side of pan.

Cover and braise for 30 minutes. Turn potatoes and yams and add just enough broth to keep them moist. Braise until potatoes, yams, and turkey are fork-tender, about 30 minutes more, adding broth as needed. Remove to a warmed platter, garnish with parsley and remaining rosemary, and serve.

To prepare: 15 minutes

To cook: 1 hour 40 minutes

4 servings

fresh crab salad with orange & tangerine

3 cups (9 oz/280 g) finely shredded green cabbage

1 Tbsp canola oil

2 tsp rice wine vinegar

½ lb (250 g) fresh lump crabmeat

4 oranges

2 tangerines

2 serrano chiles, seeded and minced

2 Tbsp finely chopped red onion

¼ cup (⅓ oz/10 g) chopped fresh cilantro (fresh coriander), plus sprigs for garnish (optional)

2 Tbsp lime juice

2 avocados, peeled, pitted, and diced

In a bowl, toss cabbage with oil and vinegar. Set aside.

Pick over crabmeat for bits of shell or cartilage. Set aside.

Slice off top and bottom of each orange and tangerine. Stand fruit upright and cut away peel, pith, and membrane, following curve of fruit. Cut along each side of membrane between sections, letting them drop into a bowl. Cut each section in half crosswise.

Put citrus sections in a bowl with chiles, onion, chopped cilantro, lime juice, ½ teaspoon salt, and ½ teaspoon pepper. Stir well. Gently stir in avocados.

To serve, divide cabbage among plates. Top with citrus mixture and crabmeat. Garnish with cilantro sprigs, if desired.

To prepare: 40 minutes

4 servings

pumpkin gratin with golden bread crumbs

3 tsp butter

4 lb (2 kg) Sugar Pie pumpkin or butternut squash, seeded and cut into wedges 2 inches (5 cm) thick

2 Tbsp olive oil

½ tsp freshly grated nutmeg

¼ cup (2 oz/60 g) crème fraîche

¼ cup (½ oz/15 g) fresh bread crumbs

1 tsp minced fresh rosemary

2 Tbsp grated Parmesan cheese

2 Tbsp shredded Gruyère cheese

Preheat oven to 350°F (180°C). Grease a baking dish with 2 tsp of butter.

Coat pumpkin with olive oil and place on a baking sheet. Bake until tender, about 1½ hours. Remove from oven, scoop out flesh, and discard skin. Put flesh in a bowl with nutmeg, 1 tsp salt, ½ tsp pepper, and crème fraîche. Mix well. Spread in prepared baking dish. Melt remaining butter in a frying pan over medium heat. Add bread crumbs and stir until golden, about 2 minutes. Sprinkle crumbs, rosemary, and cheeses over pumpkin. Bake until slightly golden on top and bubbling at edges, about 20 minutes more. Serve at once.

Note: Serve with Braised Mixed Greens, page 44.

To prepare: 20 minutes

To cook: 1 hour 50 minutes

4–6 servings

duck breasts stuffed with dried pears & apricots

2 duck breast halves

Stuffing

2 Tbsp finely chopped white onion

2 dried pears, finely chopped

4 dried apricots, finely chopped

2 Tbsp chopped walnuts

1 tsp paprika

¼ cup (2 fl oz/60 ml) sweet vermouth

¼ cup (2 fl oz/60 ml) low-sodium chicken broth

Remove skin and fat from duck by pulling fatty layer back and cutting it from meat with a small knife. Set breast aside. Place fatty layer, skin side down, in a frying pan over medium heat. Cook, turning occasionally, until about 2 Tbsp fat is rendered, 7–10 minutes. Discard skin. Pour off and reserve all but 1 tsp of fat.

For Stuffing: Return pan to medium heat, add onion, and sauté until translucent, about 2 minutes. Add pears, apricots, and walnuts and sauté until blended, 3–4 minutes. Remove from heat and set aside.

With a sharp knife, slit duck breast lengthwise through center to make a deep pocket. Rub duck inside and out with paprika, 1 tsp salt, and 1 tsp pepper. Spoon stuffing into pocket. Do not overstuff. Stuffing should reach edges of pocket, but pocket should close; if needed, use tooth-picks to secure opening.

Heat 1 Tbsp reserved duck fat in a frying pan over medium-high heat. Add stuffed breast and sear for 1–2 minutes. Reduce heat to medium and cook until browned, about 4 minutes more. Push back any errant stuffing with back of a spatula and carefully turn breast. Cook on second side until browned, about 4 minutes. Carefully remove to a cutting board, tent with foil, and let rest.

Heat pan drippings over medium-high heat. Add vermouth and stir to scrape up browned bits. Add broth, reduce heat to medium, and simmer until liquid is reduced to 2–3 Tbsp, 5–6 minutes.

To serve, cut duck breast crosswise into slices ½ inch (12 mm) thick. (Stuffing will fall out a bit.) Arrange slices on warmed plates, tucking in stuffing as necessary. Drizzle with pan sauce and serve immediately.

Note: Serve with arugula (rocket) salad.

To prepare: 30 minutes

To cook: 30 minutes

3 or 4 servings

rhubarb cranberries red onions

RED FRUITS AND VEGETABLES PROVIDE ANTIOXIDANTS

ruby grapefruit radishes beets

FOR PROTECTION AND HEALING • PROMOTE HEART

cherries watermelon red plums

HEALTH • PROMOTE URINARY TRACT HEALTH • HELP

tomatoes red pears raspberries

REDUCE THE RISK OF CERTAIN CANCERS • IMPROVE

pomegranates red bell peppers

MEMORY FUNCTION • RED FRUITS AND VEGETABLES

radicchio strawberries quinces

OFFER ANTIOXIDANTS FOR PROTECTION AND HEALING

Red

Just as the color green brings an instant association with vegetables, red conjures a world of fruits, from crisp apples to juicy strawberries. Red vegetables, such as spicy radishes or pleasantly bitter radicchio, are no less appealing and nutritious. And one of the most beneficial red foods, the tomato, is a sort of hybrid: botanically a fruit, it is commonly thought of and prepared as a vegetable.

Tomatoes are particularly rich in lycopene, a powerful antioxidant found in red produce. Summer, when cherry tomatoes are at their peak, is the time to make a frittata with an abundance of these sweet gems (page 102). Another warm-weather treat is sautéed sweet red bell pepper (capsicum), partnered with whole-wheat (wholemeal) pasta, and enriched with a dusting of Parmesan (page 96) to make a meatless main course.

Pears and cheese are a classic after-dinner combination. But when diced red-skinned pear and a judicious amount of pungent Gorgonzola cheese are stirred into a creamy risotto (page 99), they prove they are ready to make a dinnertime debut.

Red fruits make delicious complements to meat and poultry. Fresh raspberries practically melt into a pan sauce served with Cornish hens (page 95). Rhubarb is cooked with spices and lemon zest into an exotic-tasting chutney served on pork medallions (page 96), but which could pair just as well with chicken or duck.

SPRING	SUMMER	AUTUMN	WINTER
beets	cherries	red apples	red apples
pink or red grapefruit	red bell peppers	beets	beets
red onions	red chiles	red bell peppers	cranberries
blood oranges	red onions	red chiles	pink or red grapefruit
red potatoes	red plums	cranberries	red grapes
radicchio	radishes	red grapes	blood oranges
radishes	raspberries	red pears	pomegranates
rhubarb	strawberries	red plums	red potatoes
strawberries	tomatoes	pomegranates	quinces
	watermelon	quinces	radicchio
		red potatoes	radishes
		raspberries	

game hens with raspberry-wine sauce

2 Cornish hens, 14–16 oz (440–500 g) each

1 Tbsp olive oil

1 Tbsp Dijon mustard

1 Tbsp raspberry vinegar

2 tsp minced fresh thyme, plus 6 sprigs

2 tsp minced shallot

⅓ cup (3 fl oz/80 ml) dry white wine

1 tsp balsamic vinegar

1¾ cups (7 oz/220 g) raspberries

¼ cup (2 fl oz/60 ml) low-sodium chicken broth

Preheat oven to 350°F (180°C). Remove giblets from hens and reserve for another use. Pat hens dry inside and out with paper towels. Coat with oil.

Stir mustard, raspberry vinegar, minced thyme, 1 tsp salt, and 1 tsp pepper together in a small bowl. Brush hens with mixture. Tuck 3 thyme sprigs into body cavity of each hen. Place on a rack in a roasting pan and roast until juices run clear when an inner thigh is pierced with a knife, about 1 hour. Remove to a carving board and tent with foil.

Pour off all but 1 tsp fat from roasting pan. Place pan on stove top over medium-high heat and add shallot. Cook until translucent, about 1 minute. Add wine and stir to scrape up browned bits. Stir in balsamic vinegar and all but 12 raspberries. Reduce heat to medium and cook until berries dissolve and sauce thickens, about 4 minutes. Add broth, raise heat to high, and cook for 1 minute. Remove and strain through a fine-mesh sieve.

Using poultry scissors, cut each game hen in half. To serve, place a half hen, cut side down, on each warmed plate. Drizzle raspberry sauce around hens. Serve at once, garnished with reserved raspberries.

To prepare: 30 minutes

To cook: 65 minutes

4 servings

red bell pepper & whole-wheat pasta

¼ cup (2 fl oz/60 ml) olive oil

½ cup (2 oz/60 g) chopped yellow onion

2 cloves garlic, minced

1 large red bell pepper (capsicum), seeded and diced

12 oz (375 g) whole-wheat (wholemeal) fettuccine or other strand pasta

2 tsp minced fresh oregano

¼ cup (1 oz/30 g) shaved or grated Parmesan cheese (optional)

Heat oil in a frying pan over medium-high heat. Add onion and sauté until translucent, 2–3 minutes. Reduce heat to medium and add garlic and bell pepper. Cook, stirring occasionally, until bell pepper is soft, 7–8 minutes. Set aside.

Meanwhile, cook pasta in a large pot of salted boiling water until al dente, 10–12 minutes. Drain. Remove to a warmed bowl and stir in bell pepper mixture. Stir in half of the oregano, 1 tsp salt, and ¼ tsp pepper. Taste and adjust seasoning. Sprinkle with cheese (if using) and remaining oregano. Serve at once.

To prepare: 20 minutes:

To cook: 12 minutes

4 servings

pork medallions & rhubarb chutney

4 rhubarb stalks

1-inch (2.5-cm) piece fresh ginger

1 cup (7 oz/220 g) packed brown sugar

½ cup (4 fl oz/125 ml) cider vinegar

1 Tbsp grated lemon zest

1 cinnamon stick

¼ cup (1½ oz/45 g) golden raisins (sultanas)

2 Tbsp chopped walnuts

1 boneless pork tenderloin, about 1¼ lb (625 g), cut into slices ½ inch (12 mm) thick

½ tsp minced fresh thyme

1½ tsp freshly ground star anise

1 Tbsp olive oil

½ cup (4 fl oz/125 ml) dry white wine

Cut rhubarb into 1-inch (2.5-cm) pieces. Peel and mince ginger, and set rhubarb and ginger aside.

Combine sugar, vinegar, and lemon zest in a nonreactive saucepan and cook over low heat, stirring, until sugar dissolves, about 5 minutes. Add rhubarb, ginger, and cinnamon stick. Raise heat to medium and cook, stirring often, until rhubarb is soft, about 15 minutes. Remove cinnamon stick and add raisins, walnuts, and ⅛ tsp salt. Cook until flavors are blended, 3–4 minutes. Remove from heat and let chutney cool.

In a bowl, toss pork with thyme, star anise, 1 tsp salt, and 1 tsp pepper. Heat oil in a frying pan over medium-high heat. Add pork and sauté until lightly browned, 2–3 minutes per side. Remove to a platter and keep warm. Add wine to pan and stir to scrape up browned bits. Cook, stirring, until reduced to about 2 Tbsp, 5–7 minutes. Drizzle pan juices over pork. Top each slice of pork with ½–1 tsp chutney. Reserve remaining chutney for another use.

Note: Serve with Mashed Parsnips (page 62).

To prepare: 30 minutes

To cook: 30 minutes

3 or 4 servings

red onion & goat cheese tartlets

Pastry

1¼ cups (6½ oz/200 g) all-purpose (plain) flour

½ tsp salt

½ cup (4 oz/125 g) cold butter, cut into small pieces

2–3 Tbsp ice water

5 oz (155 g) soft goat cheese blended with 2 tsp minced fresh thyme

¼ cup (1 oz/30 g) finely chopped red onion, plus thin slices for garnish

2 tsp pink peppercorns

1 Tbsp low-fat or whole milk

Olive oil

Champagne vinegar

For Pastry: Combine flour and salt in a food processor. Add butter and pulse until mixture resembles peas. With machine running, gradually add ice water until dough comes together. Gather dough into a ball and divide into 4 smaller balls. Enclose each in plastic wrap and flatten into a disk. Place in freezer for 30 minutes, or refrigerate overnight.

Preheat oven to 375°F (190°C). On a lightly floured surface, roll out each disk into a round ¼ inch (6 mm) thick. Lay pastry rounds on a baking sheet. Spread one-fourth of herbed goat cheese in the center of each pastry round. Top with one-fourth of the chopped red onion and one-fourth of the pink peppercorns. Bring up edge of pastry and pleat so cheese is partially covered. Brush pastry with milk to encourage browning. Bake until pastry is golden, 15–20 minutes. Let cool 5 minutes before serving.

While tartlets bake, toss onion slices with oil and vinegar to moisten and sprinkle with salt. Let stand for 15–20 minutes, then use to garnish tarts.

To prepare: 25 minutes, plus 30 minutes to chill

To cook: 20 minutes

2–4 servings

risotto with red pear & gorgonzola

2 cups (16 fl oz/500 ml) low-sodium chicken broth

3 Tbsp butter

2 Tbsp olive oil

2 Tbsp finely chopped yellow onion

1½ cups (10½ oz/330 g) Arborio rice

3 oz (90 g) Gorgonzola cheese, cut into pieces

1 red pear, cored and diced

Combine broth and 3 cups (24 fl oz/750 ml) water in a saucepan. Bring to a gentle simmer and maintain over low heat.

Melt 2 Tbsp of butter with oil in a large, heavy saucepan over medium-high heat. Add onion and sauté until translucent, about 2 minutes. Add rice and stir until grains are well coated, about 1 minute. Add ½ cup (4 fl oz/125 ml) broth, reduce heat to medium, and stir until most of broth is absorbed. Repeat, stirring in ½ cup broth each time, until only a few Tbsp of broth remain and rice is creamy and tender but firm, 20–25 minutes. Add 1–2 Tbsp of broth and cheese and stir until cheese is melted. Stir in pear and season to taste with salt. Serve at once.

To prepare: 15 minutes

To cook: 25 minutes

4 or 5 servings

red onion & balsamic

Cut red onions into quarters, then grill
them over a hot wood or charcoal fire
until browned on each side. Drizzle with
a thick aged balsamic vinegar; serve as
an accompaniment to a meaty main dish.

radicchio & dried
cranberry salad

Make a vinaigrette of walnut oil and
fresh lemon juice in a salad bowl. Add
a handful of dried cranberries and let
plump. Add a head of radicchio, torn into
bite-sized pieces, and toss. Sprinkle with
toasted walnut halves and serve.

broiled tomatoes

Cut tomatoes in half and sprinkle them with salt, pepper, fresh bread crumbs, minced garlic, and olive oil, then broil (grill) them until a lightly browned, crusty topping forms, about 6 minutes.

marinated roasted red bell peppers

Roast red peppers (capsicums) until blackened and seal in a paper bag for 5 minutes. Remove skins; cut the peppers in half lengthwise, remove seeds and membranes, and slice into strips. Toss with olive oil, salt, and minced parsley.

fish & shellfish stew with new red potatoes

2 tsp butter

2 stalks celery, chopped

¼ cup (1 oz/30 g) finely chopped yellow onion

4 cups (32 fl oz/1 l) low-sodium chicken broth

1 bay leaf

6 small red potatoes, quartered

1½ lb (750 g) cod, halibut, and sea bass fillets

½ lb (250 g) bay scallops

1 tsp minced fresh thyme

2 Tbsp minced fresh parsley

Melt butter in a large saucepan over medium heat. Add celery and onion and sauté until onion is translucent, 2–3 minutes. Add chicken broth, bay leaf, ¼ tsp salt, and ¼ tsp pepper. Bring to a boil over high heat, reduce heat to low, and simmer for 10 minutes. Raise heat to medium, add potatoes, and cook until nearly fork-tender, about 10 minutes.

Cut fillets into 1-inch (2.5-cm) pieces and add to pan along with scallops. Cook until just opaque, 3–4 minutes. Add thyme and parsley. Taste and adjust seasoning. Ladle into warmed bowls to serve.

To prepare: 15 minutes

To cook: 30 minutes

4 servings

red cherry tomato & goat cheese frittata

6 eggs

2 Tbsp whole or low-fat milk

2 tsp minced fresh thyme

1 Tbsp butter

1 Tbsp extra-virgin olive oil

¼ onion, chopped

1 clove garlic, minced

24 red cherry tomatoes, halved

2 Tbsp soft goat cheese

1 Tbsp minced fresh basil

Beat eggs, milk, thyme, ¾ tsp salt, and ½ tsp pepper together in a large bowl until just blended. Melt butter with oil in a 10-inch (25-cm) frying pan over medium-high heat. Add onion and sauté until translucent, about 3 minutes. Add garlic and sauté until fragrant. Pour in egg mixture. Reduce heat to low and cook until eggs are set around edges, 3–4 minutes. Top with tomatoes, cut side up, and add goat cheese in tsp-sized dollops. Using a spatula, lift edges of eggs and tilt pan to let uncooked eggs run under. Cook until top is nearly set, 4–5 minutes.

Invert a plate on top of pan and, holding plate and pan firmly together with a pot holder, flip them to turn frittata out onto plate. Slide frittata into pan, cooked side up. Cook for 1–2 minutes, then invert a plate over pan and flip again. Sprinkle with basil. Serve hot or at room temperature, cut into wedges.

To prepare: 20 minutes

To cook: 20 minutes

4 servings

leg of lamb with cranberry & dried cherry sauce

Sauce

1½ cups (12 fl oz/375 ml) port

1 cup (4 oz/125 g) fresh or frozen cranberries

¼ cup (1 oz/30 g) plus 2 Tbsp dried cherries, chopped

1 tsp minced fresh thyme

Lamb

1 bone-in leg of lamb, about 4 lb (2 kg)

1 Tbsp olive oil

1 tsp fresh thyme leaves

1 tsp minced fresh rosemary

Preheat oven to 400°F (200°C).

For Sauce: Combine 1 cup (8 fl oz/250 ml) port, cranberries, cherries, and thyme in a saucepan. Bring to a boil over medium-high heat, reduce heat to low, and simmer until thickened to a light sauce, about 10 minutes. Set aside.

For Lamb: Rub lamb all over with oil, 1 tsp salt, ½ tsp pepper, thyme, and rosemary. Place in a roasting pan and roast for 15 minutes. Reduce oven temperature to 375°F (190°C) and roast lamb until skin and meat shrink back from bone and an instant-read thermometer inserted in center of meat not touching bone reads 135°F (56°C) for medium rare, about 30 minutes more. During last 10 minutes of roasting, baste with 2 Tbsp sauce. Remove to a carving board, tent with foil, and let rest for 10–15 minutes.

Pour off all but 1 Tbsp fat from roasting pan. Place pan on stove top over medium-high heat, add remaining ½ cup (4 fl oz/125 ml) port, and stir to scrape up browned bits. Cook until liquid is reduced by half, 4–5 minutes. Pour into saucepan with sauce and reheat briefly. Carve lamb into slices and serve with sauce.

To prepare: 20 minutes

To cook: 1 hour

6 servings

radicchio risotto with prosciutto

2 wedges radicchio, about ½ inch (12 mm) thick

2½ Tbsp olive oil

2 cups (16 fl oz/500 ml) low-sodium chicken broth

3 Tbsp butter

2 Tbsp minced shallot

1¼ cups (9 oz/280 g) Arborio or Carnaroli rice

½ cup (2 oz/60 g) grated Parmesan cheese

1½ oz (45 g) thinly sliced prosciutto, torn into pieces

Preheat broiler (grill). Place radicchio on broiler pan, brush with some of oil, and broil (grill) until lightly browned, about 4 minutes per side. Chop finely and set aside.

Combine broth and 2½ cups (20 fl oz/625 ml) water in a saucepan. Bring to a gentle simmer over low heat.

Melt 2 Tbsp of butter with remaining oil in a large, heavy saucepan over medium-high heat. Add shallot and sauté until translucent, about 2 minutes. Add rice and stir until grains are well coated, about 1 minute. Add ½ cup (4 fl oz/125 ml) simmering broth, reduce heat to medium, and stir until most of broth is absorbed. Repeat, stirring in ½ cup broth each time, until only a few Tbsp of broth remain and rice is creamy and tender but firm, 20–25 minutes. Add 1–2 Tbsp of broth and stir in remaining butter, Parmesan cheese, salt to taste, radicchio, and prosciutto, reserving some radicchio and prosciutto for garnish if desired.

Spoon risotto into warmed pasta bowls and garnish with radicchio and prosciutto if desired. Serve at once.

To prepare: 25 minutes

To cook: 35 minutes

4 servings

soybeans brown rice garbanzos

WHOLE GRAINS, LEGUMES, SEEDS, AND NUTS PROMOTE

pecans chestnuts bulgur wheat

ARTERY AND HEART HEALTH • HELP REDUCE THE RISK

flaxseed sesame seeds polenta

OF DIABETES • REDUCE HIGH BLOOD PRESSURE • OFFER

pumpkin seeds cashews quinoa

ANTIOXIDANTS FOR PROTECTION AND HEALING • HELP

kasha macadamia nuts walnuts

REDUCE THE RISK OF STROKE • MAY REDUCE THE RISK

hazelnuts oats couscous millet

OF CANCERS OF THE BREAST, PROSTATE, AND COLON

Brown

The color may not be as vivid and alluring as those in previous chapters, but the foods in the brown group are stalwarts of the healthful diet and worthy of equal respect. Grains, legumes, seeds, and nuts, regardless of their color, earn high marks for nutrient value when eaten in their unrefined "brown" state—and high praise for rich taste and hearty texture.

While many of the foods in this color group are brown, the category includes others that are yellow (polenta), dark red (kidney beans), and black (black beans). Classifying all these foods as brown underscores the importance of using them in their pure forms for the greatest nutritional value. Whole grains, for instance, are preferable to refined, and unsalted nuts are more desirable since they let you control the seasoning in a dish.

Scallops dress up a classic tabbouleh made with bulgur (page 114). Brown rice studded with nuts, fruit, and chicken makes a toothsome main-dish salad (page 120).

Legumes, a category that includes beans and peas and also peanuts, offer many of the same benefits as grains—and are just as versatile. Tiny Puy lentils make a perfect bed for salmon fillets (page 117). Split peas are the main ingredient in a soup flavored with ham and garnished with croutons (page 124), hearty enough for a main dish. And keep in mind that nuts and seeds used as garnishes enhance the nutrition of any dish.

GRAINS	LEGUMES	SEEDS	NUTS
barley	black beans	flaxseed	almonds
bulgur wheat	cannellini beans	pumpkin seeds	Brazil nuts
couscous (wheat pasta)	chickpeas	sesame seeds	cashews
kasha (buckwheat grouts)	kidney beans	sunflower seeds	chestnuts
millet	lima beans		hazelnuts
oats	soybeans		macadamia nuts
polenta (ground corn)	black-eyed peas		pecans
quinoa	split peas		pine nuts
brown rice	lentils		pistachio nuts
whole wheat	peanuts		walnuts

peanut pad thai

8 oz (250 g) rice stick noodles
(¼ inch/6 mm wide)

¼ cup (2 fl oz/60 ml) lemon juice

2 serrano chiles, seeded and minced

3 Tbsp Thai fish sauce

2 Tbsp rice wine vinegar

3 Tbsp sugar

1 tsp tomato paste

3 Tbsp canola or other vegetable oil

2 cloves garlic, minced

4 oz (125 g) firm tofu, cut into
½-inch (12-mm) cubes

8 dried shrimp (prawns), crumbled
(optional)

¼ cup (1½ oz/45 g) dried salted radish,
finely chopped (optional)

2 eggs

2 cups (4 oz/125 g) fresh bean sprouts

½ cup (⅔ oz/20 g) coarsely chopped
fresh cilantro (fresh coriander)

½ cup (3 oz/90 g) chopped unsalted
roasted peanuts

6 green (spring) onions, quartered
lengthwise and cut into 1-inch
(2.5 cm) lengths

2 limes, quartered

Put noodles in a bowl and cover with warm water.

In a small bowl, combine lemon juice, chiles, and 1 Tbsp fish sauce. In another bowl, mix vinegar, sugar, tomato paste, and remaining 2 Tbsp fish sauce together to make a seasoning mix.

Heat oil in a wok over medium-high heat until smoking. Add garlic and stir-fry for about 10 seconds. Add tofu, dried shrimp (if using), and radish (if using) and stir-fry for 1–2 minutes. Stir in seasoning mix. Break 1 egg into the wok and stir. Drain noodles and add them to wok, tossing all ingredients together. Make a well in noodles and break in second egg. Let cook until firm, about 30 seconds. Toss again. Add half of bean sprouts, half of cilantro, half of peanuts, green onions, and lemon juice mixture. Toss and cook for 30 seconds.

Remove to a platter. Garnish with remaining bean sprouts, cilantro, and peanuts, and limes quarters. Serve hot.

To prepare: 30 minutes

To cook: 5 minutes

4 servings

tabbouleh with lemony scallops

1 cup (6 oz/185 g) bulgur wheat

2 cups (16 fl oz/500 ml) boiling water

1 cup (1 oz/30 g) *each* minced fresh parsley and minced fresh dill

½ red onion, finely chopped

2 red tomatoes, finely chopped

⅓ cup (3 fl oz/80 ml) extra-virgin olive oil

⅔ cup (5 fl oz/160 ml) lemon juice

1¼ lb (20 oz/625 g) bay scallops

½ cup (2½ oz/75 g) all-purpose (plain) flour

1 Tbsp butter, or as needed

Put bulgur in a bowl and pour in boiling water. Cover and let stand for 30 minutes. Drain, pressing bulgur gently with back of a wooden spoon. Remove to a bowl and add parsley, dill, onion, tomatoes, oil, ⅓ cup (3 fl oz/80 ml) of lemon juice, ½ tsp salt, and ½ tsp pepper. Cover and refrigerate for at least 2 hours or as long as overnight.

Pat scallops dry with paper towels. Spread flour on a plate, sprinkle with ½ tsp salt and ½ tsp pepper, and lightly dust scallops. Melt butter in a large frying pan over medium-high heat. Working in batches, sear scallops in one layer without crowding until golden brown, 1–2 minutes per side. Remove to a platter and keep warm. Add remaining lemon juice to pan and stir to scrape up browned bits. Add ¼ cup (2 fl oz/60 ml) water and simmer until thickened. Serve tabbouleh accompanied with scallops and sauce.

To prepare: 30 minutes, plus 2 hours to chill

To cook: 7 minutes

4 or 5 servings

stir-fried beef with black bean sauce

¾ lb (12 oz/375 g) beef sirloin

3 Tbsp canola oil

3 Tbsp finely chopped yellow onion

2 cloves garlic, minced

6 cups (6 oz/185 g) packed spinach leaves (about 1 bunch)

2 Tbsp black bean sauce

¼ cup (2 fl oz/60 ml) sherry

2 Tbsp low-sodium beef broth

Sesame seeds for garnish

Steamed brown rice for serving

Cut beef into strips 2 inches (5 cm) long and ¼ inch (6 mm) thick.

Heat oil in a wok over high heat until almost smoking. Add onion and stir-fry for 30 seconds. Add garlic and stir-fry for 30 seconds. Add beef and stir-fry until no longer red, about 3 minutes. Using a wire skimmer, remove to a bowl.

Add spinach to wok and stir-fry until wilted, about 1 minute. Stir in black bean sauce, sherry, and beef broth. Return meat to wok and stir-fry for 1 minute to heat through and coat with sauce. Serve hot, garnished with sesame seeds and accompanied with steamed rice.

To prepare: 25 minutes

To cook: 7 minutes

4 servings

salmon fillets with puy lentils

1½ cups (10½ oz/330 g) Puy lentils

1½ Tbsp olive oil

2 Tbsp minced shallot or yellow onion

4 salmon fillets, 4 oz (125 g) each

1 cup (1 oz/30 g) mixed salad greens or arugula (rocket) (optional)

Pick over lentils, then rinse well. Heat 1 Tbsp oil in a saucepan over high heat. Add shallot and lentils and stir until shallot is translucent and lentils glisten, about 2 minutes. Add 4 cups (32 fl oz/1 l) water and ½ tsp salt. Bring to a boil, reduce heat to medium-low, cover, and simmer until lentils are tender but firm and most water is absorbed, 30–35 minutes. Remove from heat and drain well. Return to pan and cover to keep warm. Taste and adjust salt.

Meanwhile, place rack in upper third of oven and preheat to 500°F (260°C). Rub salmon fillets on both sides with remaining olive oil, salt, and pepper. Lightly grease a baking dish just large enough to hold salmon in a single layer. Roast fish until it flakes easily with a fork and is still translucent only in center, 13–15 minutes.

To serve, divide lentils among plates and top each bed of lentils with a fillet. Garnish with salad greens, if using. Serve at once.

To prepare: 20 minutes

To cook: 25 minutes

4 servings

broiled chicken thighs with sage polenta

1 cup (5 oz/155 g) fine- or medium-grind polenta

1 Tbsp minced fresh sage

1 tsp extra-virgin olive oil

4 skinless, boneless chicken thighs

3 Tbsp shredded Gruyère or grated Parmesan cheese

Bring 4 cups (32 fl oz/1 l) water to a boil in a large saucepan over high heat. Add 1 Tbsp salt and gradually stir in polenta. Reduce heat to low, add sage and ½ tsp pepper, and cook, stirring, until polenta begins to pull away from sides of pan, 8–10 minutes. Grease a 9-inch (23-cm) pie pan with oil and pour polenta into it. Set aside to cool.

Meanwhile, preheat broiler (grill). Season chicken with 1 tsp salt and 1 tsp pepper. Place on a baking sheet and slide under broiler about 6 inches (15 cm) from heat source. Broil (grill) until opaque throughout, 12–15 minutes. Remove and tent with foil.

Sprinkle polenta with cheese and slide under broiler until cheese melts and forms a light crust, about 5 minutes.

Cut polenta into wedges and chicken into strips 1 inch (2.5 cm) wide. Scatter chicken strips over polenta wedges and serve.

To prepare: 15 minutes

To cook: 20 minutes

4 servings

pearl barley & mushrooms

Simmer ½ cup (4 oz/125 g) pearl barley in 2 cups (16 fl oz/500 ml) salted water until tender, 45 minutes. Heat olive oil in a pan, add sliced mushrooms and minced shallot, and sauté well. Add barley to heat through and garnish with parsley.

puréed lentils

Cook brown lentils in salted boiling water until soft, about 20 minutes. Drain and purée in a blender or food processor with 1 Tbsp of olive oil, ½ peeled roasted red bell pepper (capsicum), salt, and pepper. Serve with flatbread.

kidney bean
& tarragon salad

Drain and rinse canned kidney beans. In a
large bowl, make a vinaigrette with extra-
virgin olive oil, champagne vinegar, and
mustard. Add the drained beans, minced
fresh tarragon, finely chopped red onion,
salt, and pepper. Mix to combine.

kasha

Mix 1 cup (8 oz/250 g) kasha with a well-
beaten egg, then sauté it in 1 Tbsp olive
oil in a hot pan to separate and toast
grains. Add 2 cups (16 fl oz/500 ml) water
and a little salt, cover, and cook until fluffy,
15 minutes. Garnish with parsley.

chicken & brown rice salad with dates & cashews

2 skin-on, bone-in chicken breast halves, 10 oz (315 g) each

2 cups (14 oz/440 g) brown rice

2 tangerines

3 Tbsp extra-virgin olive oil

2 Tbsp lemon juice

1 tsp red wine vinegar

1 tsp sugar

20 dates, pitted and coarsely chopped

½ cup (3 oz/90 g) chopped cashews

¼ cup (⅓ oz/10 g) torn fresh mint

To prepare: 30 minutes

To cook: 50 minutes

4 servings

Preheat oven to 350°F (180°C).

Rub each chicken breast on both sides with ½ tsp salt and ½ tsp pepper. Place in a baking dish and bake until skin is crisp and meat is opaque throughout, about 45 minutes. Remove and let cool. Remove skin and discard. Pull meat from bone and cut into bite-sized pieces.

Meanwhile, combine 4 cups (32 fl oz/1 l) water and 2 tsp salt in a saucepan and bring to a boil over high heat. Add rice, return to a boil, reduce heat to low, cover, and simmer until rice is tender and all water is absorbed, about 50 minutes. Remove rice from heat and let cool to room temperature.

Slice off top and bottom of each tangerine. Stand tangerine upright and cut away peel, pith, and membrane, following curve of fruit. Cut along each side of membrane between sections, letting them drop into a bowl. Cut sections in half crosswise.

In a serving bowl, combine rice, oil, lemon juice, vinegar, sugar, 2 tsp salt, and 1 tsp pepper. Stir gently with a wooden spoon. Gently stir in chicken, tangerines, most of chopped dates, half of chopped cashews, and all but 2 tsp mint. Garnish salad with remaining dates, cashews, and mint. Serve at room temperature.

couscous with peas & mint

1½ lb (750 g) fresh English peas, shelled, or ¾ cup (4 oz/125 g) frozen petite peas

1 mint sprig

Couscous

3 Tbsp butter

2 cups (12 oz/375 g) instant couscous

¼ cup (1½ oz/45 g) dried currants

⅓ cup (½ oz/15 g) minced fresh mint

If using fresh peas, bring a large saucepan of boiling water to a boil over high heat. Add peas, mint sprig, and ½ tsp salt. Reduce heat to medium and cook until peas are tender, 12–20 minutes, depending on size. Drain and set aside. Discard mint. If using frozen peas, cook in 2 Tbsp boiling water with mint sprig and ½ tsp salt until tender, about 2 minutes.

For Couscous: Combine 2 cups (16 fl oz/500 ml) water, butter, and 1 tsp salt in a saucepan and bring to a boil over high heat. Remove from heat, add couscous and currants, and let stand for 5 minutes. Turn couscous onto a platter and fluff with a fork. Fold in peas and minced mint. Serve hot or at room temperature.

Note: Serve with Baked Acorn Squash (page 81).

To prepare: 20 minutes

To cook: 25 minutes

4 servings

quinoa with tomatoes & grilled shrimp

1 cup (6 oz/185 g) quinoa

1½ lb (750 g) red and yellow tomatoes, chopped

2–3 tsp balsamic vinegar

1 cup (1½ oz/45 g) chopped fresh basil, plus sprigs for garnish

2 tsp olive oil

1 clove garlic, minced

1¼ lb (20 oz/625 g) jumbo shrimp (prawns), peeled and deveined

4 lemon wedges

Build a hot wood or charcoal fire in a grill, or preheat a gas grill to 400°F (200°C). Meanwhile, bring 2 cups (16 fl oz/500 ml) water to a boil in a saucepan over medium-high heat. Add quinoa and ½ tsp salt and return to a boil. Reduce heat to low, cover, and simmer until quinoa is tender, about 20 minutes. Remove to a large platter and spread in a thin layer to cool.

Spread tomatoes on quinoa. Sprinkle with balsamic vinegar, chopped basil, and ½ tsp pepper. Stir olive oil, garlic, shrimp, and ½ tsp salt together in a bowl.

Put shrimp in an oiled grill basket and grill until evenly bright pink, about 2 minutes per side. Remove from basket and arrange around edges of quinoa. Garnish with basil sprigs and lemon wedges and serve.

To prepare: 20 minutes

To cook: 25 minutes

4 servings

split pea & ham soup
with garlic croutons

1 ham hock

1½ cups (10½ oz/330 g) split peas

½ carrot, finely chopped

1 stalk celery, finely chopped

**¼ cup (1 oz/30 g) finely chopped
yellow onion**

1 parsley sprig

Croutons

3 Tbsp olive oil

**3 thick slices country-style bread, cut
into 1-inch (2.5-cm) cubes**

2 cloves garlic

Put ham hock in a saucepan with water to cover by 2 inches (5 cm). Bring to a boil over medium-high heat, reduce heat to low, cover, and simmer until meat is tender and falling off bone, about 1 hour. Remove meat and reserve ¼ cup (2 fl oz/60 ml) of cooking liquid. Pull meat from bone and shred or dice.

Meanwhile, in a heavy saucepan, combine 5 cups (40 fl oz/1.25 l) water, split peas, carrot, celery, onion, parsley, 1 tsp salt, and ½ tsp pepper. Bring to a boil over medium-high heat, reduce heat to low, cover, and simmer until peas are nearly falling apart, vegetables are tender, and soup is thick, about 1 hour. Remove parsley and discard. Add ham and reserved cooking liquid. Simmer for 10 minutes.

For Croutons: While the soup is simmering, heat oil in a frying pan over medium-high heat. Add bread cubes and garlic and fry, turning often, until golden, 3–4 minutes. Discard garlic and remove croutons to paper towels to drain.

To serve, ladle soup into warmed bowls and garnish with croutons.

To prepare: 20 minutes

To cook: 1 hour

4 servings

chickpea, corn
& cilantro salad

**1 can (15 oz/470 g) chickpeas
(garbanzo beans)**

Kernels cut from 4 ears white corn

¼ red onion, finely chopped

**¼ cup (⅓ oz/10 g) minced cilantro
(fresh coriander)**

**¼ tsp *each* ground cumin
and paprika**

2 Tbsp red wine vinegar

2 tsp extra-virgin olive oil

1 tsp freshly squeezed lemon juice

Drain and rinse chickpeas, then drain again. Place in a large bowl. Add corn kernels, onion, and cilantro to chickpeas.

In a small bowl, stir cumin, paprika, vinegar, olive oil, lemon juice, ½ tsp salt, and ½ tsp pepper together with a fork to make a vinaigrette.

Pour vinaigrette over vegetables and toss to coat completely. Serve at room temperature.

To prepare: 20 minutes

4–6 servings

Nutrients at work

Humans need more than forty nutrients to support life. Many foods are good sources of many different nutrients, but no single food provides everything. Eating a variety of foods, preferably in their whole form, is the best way to get all the nutrients your body needs. Some nutrients require others for optimal absorption, but excessive amounts may result in heath problems.

Until recently, nutrition experts recommended the distribution of carbohydrates, protein, and fat in a well-balanced diet to be 55 percent of calories from carbohydrates, 15 percent of calories from protein, and 30 percent of calories from fat. As we have learned more about individual health needs and differences in metabolism, we have become more flexible in determining what constitutes a healthy diet. The table below shows macronutrient ranges recommended in September 2002 by the Institute of Medicine, part of the U.S. National Academies. These ranges are more likely to accommodate everyone's health needs. To help you evaluate and balance your diet as you prepare the recipes in this book, turn to pages 130–33 for nutritional analyses of each recipe.

Nutrition experts have also determined guidelines for vitamins and minerals. For more information, see pages 128–29.

CARBOHYDRATES, PROTEIN, AND FATS

NUTRIENTS AND FOOD SOURCES	FUNCTIONS	RECOMMENDED % OF DAILY CALORIES AND GUIDANCE
Carbohydrates COMPLEX CARBOHYDRATES • Grains, breads, cereals, pastas • Dried beans and peas, lentils • Starchy vegetables (potatoes, corn, green peas)	• Main source of energy for the body • Particularly important for the brain and nervous system • Fiber aids normal digestion	45–65% • Favor complex carbohydrates, especially legumes, vegetables, and whole grains (brown rice; whole-grain bread, pasta, and cereal). • Many foods high in complex carbohydrates are also good fiber sources. Among the best are bran cereals, canned and dried beans, dried fruit, and rolled oats. Recommended daily intake of fiber for adults under age 50 is 25 g for women and 38 g for men. For women over age 50, intake is 21 g; for men, 30 g.
SIMPLE CARBOHYDRATES • Naturally occurring sugars in fruits, vegetables, and milk • Added refined sugars in soft drinks, candy, baked goods, jams and jellies, etc.	• Provide energy	• Fruit and vegetables have naturally occurring sugars but also have vitamins, minerals, and phytochemicals. Refined sugar, on the other hand, has little to offer in the way of nutrition, so limit your intake to get the most from your daily calories.

Source: Institute of Medicine. Dietary Reference Intakes for Energy, Carbohydrates, Fiber, Fat, Protein and Amino Acids (Macronutrients).

NUTRIENTS AND FOOD SOURCES	FUNCTIONS	RECOMMENDED % OF DAILY CALORIES AND GUIDANCE
Protein • Foods from animal sources • Dried beans and peas, nuts • Grain products	• Builds and repairs cells • Regulates body processes by providing components for enzymes, hormones, fluid balance, nerve transmission	10–35% • Choose lean sources such as dried beans, fish, poultry, lean cuts of meat, soy, and low-fat dairy products most of the time. • Egg yolks are rich in many nutrients but also high in cholesterol; limit to 5 per week.
Fats All fats are mixtures of saturated and unsaturated (polyunsaturated and monounsaturated) types. Polyunsaturated and especially monounsaturated types are more desirable because they promote cardiovascular health.	• Supplies essential fatty acids needed for various body processes and to build cell membranes, particularly of the brain and nervous system • Transports certain vitamins	20–35% • Experts disagree about the ideal amount of total fat in the diet. Some say more is fine if it is heart-healthy fat; others recommend limiting total fat. Virtually all experts agree that saturated fat, trans fats, and cholesterol, all of which can raise "bad" (LDL) cholesterol, should be limited.
PRIMARILY SATURATED • Foods from animal sources (meat fat, butter, cheese, cream) • Coconut, palm, palm kernel oils	• Raises blood levels of "bad" (LDL) cholesterol	• Limit saturated fat.
PRIMARILY POLYUNSATURATED (PUFA) • Omega-3 fatty acids: herring, salmon, mackerel, lake trout, sardines, sword fish, nuts, flaxseed, canola oil, soy bean oil, tofu • Omega-6: vegetable oils such as corn, soybean, and safflower (abundant in the American diet)	• Reduces inflammation, influences blood clotting and blood vessel activity to improve blood flow	• Eat fish at least twice a week. • Substitute PUFA for saturated fat or trans fat when possible.
PRIMARILY MONOUNSATURATED (MUFA) Olive oil, canola oil, sesame oil, avocados, almonds, chicken fat	• Raises blood levels of "good" (HDL) cholesterol	• Substitute MUFA for saturated fat or trans fat when possible.
DIETARY CHOLESTEROL Foods from animal sources (egg yolks, organ meats, cheese, fish roe, meat)	• A structural component of cell membranes and some hormones	• The body makes cholesterol, and some foods contain dietary cholesterol. U.S. food labels list cholesterol values.
Trans fat Processed foods, purchased baked goods, margarine and shortening	• Raises blood levels of "bad" (LDL) cholesterol	• U.S. food labels list trans fats.

FAT-SOLUBLE VITAMINS AND FOOD SOURCES	FUNCTIONS	DAILY RECOMMENDED INTAKES FOR ADULTS*
Vitamin A Dairy products, deep yellow-orange fruits and vegetables, dark green leafy vegetables, liver, fish, fortified milk, cheese, butter	• Promotes growth and healthy skin and hair • Helps build strong bones and teeth • Works as an antioxidant that may reduce the risk of some cancers and other diseases • Helps night vision • Increases immunity	700 mcg for women 900 mcg for men
Vitamin D Fortified milk, salmon, sardines, herring, butter, liver, fortified cereals, fortified margarine	• Builds bones and teeth • Enhances calcium and phosphorus absorption and regulates blood levels of these nutrients	5–10 mcg
Vitamin E Nuts and seeds, vegetable and seed oils (corn, soy, sunflower), whole-grain breads and cereals, dark green leafy vegetables, dried beans and peas	• Helps form red blood cells • Improves immunity • Prevents oxidation of LDL cholesterol • Works as an antioxidant that may reduce the risk of some cancers	15 mg
Vitamin K Dark green leafy vegetables, liver, carrots, asparagus, cauliflower, cabbage, wheat bran, wheat germ, eggs	• Needed for normal blood clotting • Promotes protein synthesis for bone, plasma, and organs	90 mcg for women 120 mcg for men

WATER-SOLUBLE VITAMINS

B vitamins Grain products, dried beans and peas, dark green leafy vegetables, dairy products, meat, poultry, fish, eggs, organ meats, milk, brewer's yeast, wheat germ, seeds	• Help the body use carbohydrates (biotin, B_{12}, niacin, pantothenic acid) • Regulate metabolism of cells and energy production (niacin, pantothenic acid) • Keep the nerves and muscles healthy (thiamin) • Protect against spinal birth defects (folate) • Protect against heart disease (B_6, folate)	• B_6: 1.3–1.5 mg • B_{12}: 2.4 mcg (B_{12} is found only in animal-based food sources; vegetarians need supplements.) • Biotin: 30 mcg • Niacin: 14 mg niacin equivalents for women; 16 mg for men • Pantothenic acid: 5 mg • Riboflavin: 1.1 mg for women; 1.3 mg for men • Thiamin: 1.1 mg for women; 1.2 mg for men
Vitamin C Many fruits and vegetables, especially citrus fruits, broccoli, tomatoes, green bell peppers (capsicums), melons, strawberries, potatoes, papayas	• Helps build body tissues • Fights infection and helps heal wounds • Helps body absorb iron and folate • Helps keep gums healthy • Works as an antioxidant	75 mg for women 90 mg for men

Sources: Institute of Medicine reports, 1999–2001

*mcg=micrograms; mg=milligrams

MINERALS ** AND FOOD SOURCES	FUNCTIONS	DAILY RECOMMENDED INTAKES FOR ADULTS *
Calcium Dairy products (especially hard cheese, yogurt, and milk), fortified juices, sardines and canned fish eaten with bones, shellfish, tofu (if processed with calcium), dark green leafy vegetables	• Helps build bones and teeth and keep them strong • Helps heart, muscles, and nerves work properly	1,000–1,200 mg
Iron Meat, fish, shellfish, egg yolks, dark green leafy vegetables, dried beans and peas, grain products, dried fruits	• Helps red blood cells carry oxygen • Component of enzymes • Strengthens immune system	18 mg for women 8 mg for men
Magnesium Nuts and seeds, whole grain products, dark green leafy vegetables, dried beans and peas	• Helps build bones and teeth • Helps nerves and muscles work properly • Necessary for DNA and RNA • Necessary for carbohydrate metabolism	310–320 mg for women 400–420 mg for men
Phosphorus Seeds and nuts, meat, poultry, fish, dried beans and peas, dairy products, whole-grain products, eggs, brewer's yeast	• Helps build strong bones and teeth • Has many metabolic functions • Helps body get energy from food	700 mg
Potassium Fruit, vegetables, dried beans and peas, meat, poultry, fish, dairy products, whole grains	• Helps body maintain water and mineral balance • Regulates heartbeat and blood pressure	2,000 mg suggested; no official recommended intake
Selenium Seafood, chicken, organ meats, brown rice, whole-wheat (wholemeal) bread, peanuts, onions	Works as an antioxidant with vitamin E to protect cells from damage • Boosts immune function	55 mg
Zinc Oysters, meat, poultry, fish, soybeans, nuts, whole grains, wheat germ	• Helps body metabolize proteins, carbohydrates, and alcohol • Helps wounds heal • Needed for growth, immune response, and reproduction	8 mg for women 11 mg for men

** The following minerals are generally sufficient in the diet when the minerals listed above are present: chloride, chromium, copper, fluoride, iodine, manganese, molybdenum, sodium, and sulfur. For information on functions and food sources, consult a nutrition book.

Nutritional values

The recipes in this book have been analyzed for significant nutrients to help you evaluate your diet and balance your meals throughout the day. Using these calculations, along with the other information in this book, you can create meals that have the optimal balance of nutrients. Having the following nutritional values at your fingertips will help you plan healthful meals.

Keep in mind that the calculations reflect nutrients per serving unless otherwise noted. Not included in the calculations are ingredients that are optional or added to taste, or those that are suggested as an alternative or substitution in the recipe, recipe note, or variation. For recipes that yield a range of servings, the calculations are for the middle of that range. Many recipes call for a specific amount of salt and also suggest seasoning food to taste; however, if you are on a low-sodium diet, it is prudent to omit salt. If you have particular concerns about any nutrient needs, consult your doctor.

The numbers for all nutritional values have been rounded using the guidelines required for reporting nutrient levels in the "Nutrition Facts" panel on U.S. food labels.

The best way to acquire the nutrients your body needs is through food. However, a balanced multivitamin-mineral supplement or a fortified cereal that does not exceed 100 percent of the daily need for any nutrient is a safe addition to your diet.

WHAT COUNTS AS A SERVING?	HOW MANY SERVINGS DO YOU NEED EACH DAY?		
	For a 1,600-calorie-per-day diet *(children 2–6, sedentary women, some older adults)*	For a 2,200-calorie-per-day diet *(children over 6, teen girls, active women, sedentary men)*	For a 2,800-calorie-per-day diet *(teen boys, active men)*
Fruit Group 1 medium whole fruit such as apple, orange, banana, or pear ½ cup (2–3 oz/60–90 g) chopped, cooked, or canned fruit ¼ cup (3 oz/90 g) dried fruit ¾ cup (6 fl oz/180 ml) fruit juice	2	3	4
Vegetable Group 1 cup (1 oz/30 g) raw, leafy vegetables ½ cup (2–3 oz/60–90 g) other vegetables, cooked or raw ¾ cup (6 fl oz/180 ml) vegetable juice	3	4	5
Bread, Cereal, Rice, and Pasta Group 1 slice of bread 1 cup (6 oz/180 g) ready-to-eat cereal ½ cup (2.5 oz/80 g) cooked cereal, rice, pasta	6	9	11

Adapted from USDA Dietary Guidelines (2005).

Purple & blue		CALORIES	PROTEIN/ GM	CARBS/ GM	TOT. FAT/ GM	SAT. FAT/ GM	CHOL/ MG	FIBER/ GM	SODIUM/ MG
p.23	Beef medallions with blueberry sauce	341	26	17	16	6	85	2	646
p.23	Purple asparagus & chicken stir-fry	207	25	4	10	1	63	2	158
p.24	Grilled eggplant sandwiches with aioli	641	10	69	38	4	42	6	766
p.27	Quail with roasted fresh figs	564	44	29	30	8	166	5	699
p.27	Roasted purple pepper frittata	224	13	6	16	6	332	1	655
p.30	Prune, raisin & lamb stew with almonds	459	40	32	18	4	111	4	461
p.33	Purple cabbage, apples & bratwurst	441	15	24	33	11	70	4	1363
p.33	Chicken breasts with purple grape sauce	372	32	29	11	3	83	2	689

Green		CALORIES	PROTEIN/ GM	CARBS/ GM	TOT. FAT/ GM	SAT. FAT/ GM	CHOL/ MG	FIBER/ GM	SODIUM/ MG
p.39	Shrimp, baby spinach & basil risotto	447	20	64	15	5	101	3	194
p.39	Artichokes stuffed with orzo & feta salad	384	15	57	13	4	19	11	687
p.40	Snow peas & chicken green curry	311	16	31	14	5	37	4	155
p.40	Orecchiette with spicy broccoli rabe	492	18	55	22	4	16	2	556
p.43	Pan-seared tuna with parsley relish	315	32	2	19	3	67	1	934
p.43	Chicken pockets with avocado salsa	464	25	34	27	4	47	8	648
p.46	Cod braised with bok choy	120	22	5	1	0	43	2	658
p.46	Green grape, pear & duck salad	232	11	30	9	3	42	3	623
p.49	Pork cutlets with sautéed kale	219	21	7	12	3	49	1	682
p.49	Halibut in parchment with zucchini & mint	344	23	5	26	6	82	2	281
p.50	Scallops with brussels sprouts & bacon	152	10	13	7	2	22	2	960

White & tan

		CALORIES	PROTEIN/ GM	CARBS/ GM	TOT. FAT/ GM	SAT. FAT/ GM	CHOL/ MG	FIBER/ GM	SODIUM/ MG
p.57	Mushroom galettes	544	15	41	36	19	83	5	387
p.58	Grilled chicken with white peach salsa	259	35	11	8	2	94	2	376
p.58	Grilled flank steak with white corn relish	444	37	18	25	6	67	3	953
p.61	Chicken & jerusalem artichoke soup	344	23	42	9	2	50	5	423
p.61	Cauliflower gratin	249	11	11	19	8	37	4	340
p.64	Celery root & potato potpie	442	8	49	25	15	60	5	626
p.67	Beef, ginger & white onion stir-fry	516	21	36	32	8	87	3	518
p.67	Leek & new potato stew with bockwurst	312	14	37	13	5	30	4	518
p.68	Cauliflower & potato sauté with cumin	221	5	30	10	3	8	4	610
p.68	Pork & parsnip braise	484	53	24	17	6	138	5	1091

Yellow & orange

		CALORIES	PROTEIN/ GM	CARBS/ GM	TOT. FAT/ GM	SAT. FAT/ GM	CHOL/ MG	FIBER/ GM	SODIUM/ MG
p.75	Honey-glazed lamb chops with apricot salsa	323	14	19	21	8	59	2	629
p.75	Artic char with yellow beets & horseradish sauce	248	22	10	13	3	63	3	457
p.76	Butternut squash pizza	663	16	79	32	7	14	7	1326
p.79	Salmon & yellow corn chowder with pancetta	362	25	35	15	5	61	3	706
p.79	Broiled chicken with carrot & potato purée	412	32	29	18	4	82	4	1554
p.82	Grilled trout with golden squash kebabs	281	31	4	15	3	90	1	74
p.82	Beef & carrot stew with star anise	466	35	29	15	4	73	7	797
p.85	Roast pork loin with rutabagas & apples	419	45	17	18	6	126	3	652
p.85	Slow-braised turkey thighs, potatoes & yams	513	43	39	21	4	166	4	774
p.86	Fresh crab salad with orange & tangerine	325	16	29	19	2	40	11	516
p.86	Pumpkin gratin with golden bread crumbs	225	5	21	14	6	21	2	558
p.89	Duck breasts stuffed with dried pears & apricots	181	14	14	6	1	48	2	627

Red		CALORIES	PROTEIN/ GM	CARBS/ GM	TOT. FAT/ GM	SAT. FAT/ GM	CHOL/ MG	FIBER/ GM	SODIUM/ MG
p.95	Game hens with raspberry-wine sauce	635	49	8	43	11	279	4	823
p.96	Red bell pepper & whole-wheat pasta	475	16	69	17	3	7	12	698
p.96	Pork medallions & rhubarb chutney	493	30	66	11	2	79	2	737
p.99	Red onion & goat cheese tartlets	655	16	41	48	28	107	2	991
p.99	Risotto with red pear & gorgonzola	397	10	53	18	9	33	3	283
p.102	Fish & shellfish stew with new red potatoes	278	43	17	4	1	88	2	478
p.102	Red cherry tomato & goat cheese frittata	232	13	6	17	7	334	2	602
p.105	Leg of lamb with cranberry & dried cherry sauce	433	44	14	14	5	134	1	117
p.106	Radicchio risotto with prosciutto	468	15	53	23	10	44	2	493

Brown		CALORIES	PROTEIN/ GM	CARBS/ GM	TOT. FAT/ GM	SAT. FAT/ GM	CHOL/ MG	FIBER/ GM	SODIUM/ MG
p.113	Peanut pad thai	525	16	68	22	3	106	4	1107
p.114	Tabbouleh with lemony scallops	425	25	41	19	4	43	7	663
p.114	Stir-fried beef with black bean sauce	400	20	26	23	5	58	3	139
p.117	Salmon fillets with puy lentils	483	47	49	12	2	72	10	348
p.117	Broiled chicken thighs with sage polenta	236	17	22	8	3	55	2	1807
p.120	Chicken & brown rice salad with dates & cashews	824	34	118	26	5	60	9	2391
p.123	Couscous with peas & mint	482	15	84	9	6	23	9	597
p.123	Quinoa with tomatoes & grilled shrimp	321	30	36	7	1	210	4	567
p.124	Spilt pea & ham soup with garlic croutons	480	25	65	14	3	14	2	750
p.124	Chickpea, corn & cilantro salad	136	6	22	4	0	0	4	465

Glossary

apples: The major portion of the apple's nutrition is in its skin, which contains the flavonoid quercetin, an antioxidant that fights viruses and allergies and is thought to be an anticarcinogenic. Apple flesh is an important source of pectin, a fiber that lowers cholesterol.

apricots: The apricot's color is due to the pigments beta-carotene and lycopene, which promote eye health and heart health, lower the risk of some cancers, and strengthen the immune system. Apricots are also high in vitamin C, potassium, and fiber.

artichokes: The artichoke's fleshy heart provides a complex of heart-healthy phytochemicals, including cynarin; it also contains chlorophyll and beta-carotene and provides a wide range of vitamins and minerals.

arugula (rocket): A bitter green, arugula is eaten both cooked and raw. It is a good source of iron and vitamins A and C and contains lutein, which protects eye health.

asparagus: This vegetable is one of the best sources of folate, a B vitamin that helps fight heart disease. It is also rich in phytochemicals, especially the flavonoid rutin, and a host of vitamins and minerals.

avocados: Technically a fruit, the avocado is high in fat, but most of it is monounsaturated, which helps to lower cholesterol. It also contains beta-sitosterol, a plant cholesterol that lowers cholesterol as well, and may prevent the growth of cancer cells. Avocados are high in vitamins and minerals, especially vitamins A, C, folate, B_6, and potassium.

bananas: Bananas are especially high in potassium, which balances sodium and helps regulate blood pressure, and may reduce arterial plaque formation. Potassium also helps to prevent strokes by lowering platelet activity and reducing blood clots. Bananas are also high in vitamins C and B_6, and contain a kind of fiber that may protect against colon cancer.

barley: Hulled barley, Scotch barley (coarsely ground), and grits (cracked) retain their bran and germ, and so provide the antioxidant selenium. Pearl barley, which has been refined, steamed, and polished, lacks the nutrients of these whole grains.

basil: Traditionally used in kitchens throughout the Mediterranean and in Southeast Asia, basil is one of the world's best-loved herbs and is a source of green phytonutrients. Although related to mint, basil tastes faintly of anise and cloves. Italian cooks use it in pesto, often pair it with tomatoes, and consider it essential to a classic minestrone. In Thailand and Vietnam, basil is often combined with fresh mint for seasoning stir-fries, curries, and salads.

bay leaf: Elongated gray-green leaves used to flavor sauces, soups, stews, and braises, imparting a slightly sweet, citrusy, nutty flavor. Usually sold dried, bay leaves should be removed from a dish before serving, as they are leathery and can have sharp edges.

beans, black: Also called turtle beans, these have a robust taste and are popular in Mexican cuisine. Like all dried beans, black beans contain protein, iron, calcium, and phosphorus; they are especially high in fiber.

beans, cannellini: These ivory-colored kidney beans, used in Italian cooking, have a buttery texture and a delicate taste. Great Northern beans may be substituted.

beans, kidney: Shaped like the organ that gives them their name, red kidney beans are meaty and have a more assertive flavor than white kidney beans (cannellini beans).

beets: Red beets get their color from the phytochemical betacyanin, which is believed to reduce tumor growth. They also contain betaine, which helps protect the heart, and salicic acid, which has anti-inflammatory properties, and are especially high in folate. The phytochemicals in golden beets help promote eye health and boost immunity.

Belgian endive (chicory/witloof): A member of the chicory family, Belgian endive is blanched (grown in darkness) to prevent it from turning green. It does contain phytochemicals based on the color of the tips, purple or green.

bell peppers (capsicums): All bell peppers are high in cancer-fighting phytochemicals; the various compounds that give them their different colors also promote eye health (green, yellow, orange, and red); the antioxidants in purple bell peppers aid memory function and promote healthy aging. Red peppers are high in vitamin C.

blueberries: These native American berries are so high in antioxidant and anti-inflammatory compounds that they are considered "brain food": they contain a range of anthocyanins, which are thought to help fight cancer and have antiaging capabilities. Blueberries are available fresh, dried, and frozen.

bok choy: Eaten for both its white bulb and its green leaves, bok choy is a type of cabbage and contains the same cancer-fighting compounds and a range of vitamins and minerals.

broccoli: Extremely high in vitamin C (½ cup/ 2 oz/60 g provides 68 percent of the Daily Value) and even higher in vitamin K, broccoli also contains vitamin A and cancer-fighting phytochemicals. Broccoli sprouts also contain high levels of these compounds.

broccoli rabe: With its long, thin stalks and small flowering heads, broccoli rabe has an assertive, bitter flavor. It contains many of the same nutrients as broccoli.

Brussels sprouts: These miniature green cabbages contain the same cancer-fighting compounds as their larger cousins, and are even higher in vitamin C and K than broccoli; just 4 Brussels sprouts contain 243 percent of the daily value of vitamin K, which promotes proper blood clotting.

bulgur wheat: Like other whole grains, bulgur wheat is rich in selenium, an antioxidant that is believed to fight cancer. Bulgur wheat kernels have been steamed, dried, and crushed, and are available in various grinds.

cabbage: The patriarch of the cruciferous vegetable family, cabbage is high in vitamins C and K, but its real value is its concentration of isothiocyanates, powerful cancer-fighting compounds. Red cabbage, which is actually purple, contains more vitamin C than green cabbage, along with the antioxidant anthocyanin.

capers: A Mediterranean shrub is the source of these small unopened flower buds. The buds are bitter when raw; once they are dried and packed in brine or salt, they are used to add a pleasantly pungent flavor to a variety of dishes. Capers should be rinsed before use to remove excess brine or salt.

carrots: One carrot provides a whopping 330 percent of the Daily Value of vitamin A, which is the source of its fame as a protector of eye health. Carrots are also high in fiber and the bioflavonoids and carotenoids that lower the risk of some cancers, protect the heart, and boost immunity. Maroon and purple carrots are colorful alternatives to the common orange carrot, offering different phytochemical benefits, and these colors of carrot are becoming more widely available.

cauliflower: Another member of the cruciferous family, cauliflower was traditionally blanched, or covered during growing, to keep the head white; now it has been bred to be naturally white. Even so, it still contains the cancer-fighting compounds of its cousins, along with phytochemicals that promote hearth health. Purple cauliflower offers a colorful change of pace from the common white cauliflower.

celery: Like other green vegetables, celery helps to fight certain cancers, promotes eye health, strengthens the immune system, and helps build strong bones and teeth. It is also high in fiber.

cheese, blue: These cheeses are inoculated with the spores of special molds to develop a fine network of blue veins for a strong, sharp, peppery flavor and a crumbly texture. Most blue cheeses can be crumbled, diced, spread, and sliced. Depending on the cheese's moisture content, however, some hold their shape when sliced better than others.

cheese, feta: Young cheese traditionally made from sheep's milk and used in Greek cuisine. It is known for its crumbly texture; some versions are also creamy. Feta's saltiness is heightened by the brine in which the cheese is pickled. Feta is also produced from cow's or goat's milk. Reduced-fat feta is also available.

cherries: Tart red and sweet dark red cherries derive their color from anthocyanin pigments and other antioxidants, which help protect the heart and brain, lower the risk of some cancers, and are powerful anti-inflammatories. Both sweet and tart cherries also contain a terpenoid that appears to prevent the growth of tumors.

chickpeas (garbanzo beans): These crumpled-looking dried beans are meaty and hearty-flavored when cooked. They are popular in soups and purées, and are the basis for hummus, the Middle Eastern dip.

chiles: All chiles contain the phytochemical capsaicin, which gives them their hot taste and also acts as a cancer fighter. Although usually eaten only in small amounts, they are nutrient rich, containing vitamins A, C, and E, along with folic acid and potassium.

chives: These slender, bright green stems are used to give an onionlike flavor without the bite. The slender, hollow, grasslike leaves can be snipped with a pair of kitchen scissors to any length and scattered over scrambled eggs, stews, salads, soups, tomatoes, or any dish that would benefit from a boost of mild oniony flavor. Chives do not take well to long cooking—they lose flavor and crispness and turn a dull, grayish green.

cilantro: Also called fresh coriander and Chinese parsley, cilantro is a distinctly flavored herb with legions of loyal followers. Used extensively in the cuisines of Mexico, the Caribbean, India, Egypt, Thailand, Vietnam, and China, cilantro asserts itself with a flavor that can't be missed. Some describe its taste as being citrusy or minty; others find hints of sage and parsley; some detractors describe it as soapy. It is best used fresh, added at the end of cooking, as it loses flavor after long exposure to heat.

corn: Corn is rich in vitamins, minerals, protein, and fiber. Yellow corn is given its color by carotenoids that not only fight heart disease and cancer, but also protect against macular degeneration.

couscous: A pasta made from high-protein durum wheat, couscous is also available in whole-wheat (wholemeal) form, which cooks just as quickly and is virtually indistinguishable from regular couscous.

cranberries: High in both fiber and vitamin C, cranberries are excellent for preventing urinary tract infections due to their polyphenols. The anthocyanins that make cranberries red have antioxidant properties that protect the heart and may guard against cancer. Fresh, frozen, and dried cranberries, as well as cranberry juice, are all equally beneficial to health.

crème fraîche: A soured, cultured cream product originating in France, crème fraîche is similar to sour cream. The silken, thick cream, which is 30 percent fat, is tangy and sweet, with a hint of nuttiness. It adds incomparable flavor when used as a topping for berries and pastry desserts. It is also delicious paired with smoked salmon and trout, and lends a velvety smoothness and rich flavor to soups and sauces. Crème fraîche is not always easy to find and many home cooks make their own from heavy cream and buttermilk.

cucumbers: A member of the gourd family, the most commonly available cucumber is sold with a waxed coating, which must be peeled, thus removing the beneficial phytochemicals of its skin. The unwaxed, thinner skin of English (hothouse) cucumbers can be eaten, as can that of Armenian cucumbers, similar to English cucumbers but smaller.

currants, dried black: Dried black currants are actually dried Zante grapes. Although smaller than raisins, they have most of the same nutrients.

dates: Occasionally available fresh in late summer and early fall, dates are more commonly found dried, when their high sugar content increases greatly. They also provide iron and protein.

dill: The fine, feathery leaves of this herb have a distinct aromatic flavor. Dill is used in savory pastries, baked vegetables, and, of course, in the making of pickles.

eggplants (aubergines): The purple skin of the familiar globe eggplant is rich in heart- and brain-healthy anthocyanins, while its flesh contains saponins, antioxidants that help to lower cholesterol levels. Other varieties may be slightly smaller and have lavender, white, rose, green, or variegated skin. The color of the eggplant's skin does not determine the flavor.

fennel seeds: The seed of the common fennel has a licorice-like flavor and may be used ground or whole in savory dishes such as bouillabaisse, sausage, and pork stews and roasts. It is also used in some breads and desserts and to flavor liqueurs.

figs: Whether fresh (available in summer and early fall) or dried, figs provide phosphorus, calcium, and iron.

garlic: Unusually rich in antioxidants and anti-inflammatories, garlic forms organosulfur compounds when chopped, crushed, or sliced. These substances lower blood pressure, slow clotting, and promote heart health.

ginger: Prized in Chinese cuisine for its culinary and medicinal uses, ginger aids digestion and lowers cholesterol. It contains both antioxidant and antimicrobial compounds.

grapefruit: Half a grapefruit provides 70 percent of Daily Value of vitamin C. Pink or red grapefruits are high in vitamin A as well. Both yellow and pink types contain flavonoids that help guard against cancer, while the latter also has lycopene, which boosts that activity.

grapes: The dark purple Concord grape, which is usually made into grape juice, is extremely high in antioxidants, making grape juice an important heart-healthy food. Red table grapes also promote heart health and immunity, and green grapes can help lower cancer risk and promote eye health.

green beans: Providing both vitamins A and C, green beans also protect eye health because of their lutein content.

green (spring) onions: Like all onions, green onions contain organosulfur compounds, which are thought to protect the heart and improve the good/bad cholesterol ratio.

ham, serrano: Ham is a portion of the lean hind leg of a pig that has been cured, or preserved, and flavored, often by smoking. The curing is done by various methods, depending on the style of ham. Traditional European hams, like Italian prosciutto and Spanish serrano, are dry-cured in salt and air-dried.

Jerusalem artichokes (sunchokes): Although they are not true artichokes but a kind of sunflower, these tubers have a nutty taste slightly reminiscent of artichokes. They are particularly high in iron and may be eaten either raw or cooked.

jicama: Technically a legume, crisp and nutty jicama is eaten both raw and cooked. It provides vitamin C and potassium.

juniper berries: These attractive blue-black berries, the size of small peas, are harvested from the evergreen juniper bush. They are added to marinades used to flavor assertive-tasting meats such as rabbit, lamb, and venison. Their best-known use is to flavor gin.

kale: Another member of the wide-ranging cruciferous vegetable family, kale shares their cancer-fighting abilities. A half-cup serving is high in vitamin A (96 percent of Daily Value), and contains a spectacular amount of vitamin K (590 percent of Daily Value!). It has more beta-carotene than broccoli and is an important source of lutein, which promotes eye health.

kiwifruits: Extremely high in vitamin C (two kiwifruits contain 240 percent of Daily Value, almost twice as much as an orange), these fruits are also high in folate and potassium.

kumquats: These tiny oval orange citrus fruits are like backward oranges: their peel is sweet and their flesh is sour. Often candied or used sliced as an accent or as a garnish, they are high in vitamin A, vitamin C, and potassium.

leeks: By virtue of their membership in the onion family, leeks contain organosulfur compounds, which are thought to fight cancer and heart disease. They also help improve the body's good-bad cholesterol ratio.

lemons: High in vitamin C, lemons are a flavor enhancer; add lemon juice to raw and cooked fruits and use it to replace salt at the table for vegetables and fish.

lentils: High in protein, like all beans, lentils come in a wide variety of colors. They also provide iron, phosphorus, calcium, and vitamins A and B.

lettuces: The many types of lettuce can be divided into four major groups: butterhead, crisphead, leaf, and romaine (cos). Most lettuces are high in vitamins A and C; they also provide calcium and iron. The darker the green of the lettuce, the higher the level of its beneficial phytochemicals, which include the eye-protectant lutein.

limes: High in vitamin C, like all citrus fruits, lime juice also contains lutein, which benefits eye health. The Persian lime is widely available, while the yellowish green Key lime is usually found fresh only in Florida and some specialty produce markets. The juice is available in bottles.

melons: Higher in healthful nutrients than any other melon, the cantaloupe is also rich in vitamins A and C and potassium. It is heart healthy and helps to lower the risk of cancer, thanks to its beta-carotene content. A wide variety of other orange-fleshed melons are also available. Green-fleshed honeydew melons and Persian melons contain cancer fighting phytochemicals as well.

millet: These pale yellow, spherical, mild-flavored grains are cooked in liquid and swell considerably in size to make a side dish or breakfast cereal popular in southern Europe, northern Africa, and Asia.

mint: A refreshing herb available in many varieties, with spearmint the most common. Used fresh to flavor a broad range of savory preparations, including spring lamb, poultry, and vegetables, or to garnish desserts.

mushrooms: Not vegetables or fruits but fungi, mushrooms come in a variety of forms and are available both wild and cultivated. They are rich in riboflavin, niacin, and pantothenic acid, all B-complex vitamins, and also contain the valuable minerals copper and selenium.

nectarines: A relative of the peach, the nectarine has the advantage of an edible skin that contains many of its phytochemicals. Yellow nectarines contain beta carotene, while the pink-skinned, white-fleshed variety has its own group of beneficial compounds.

nuts: High in fiber, nuts also contain folate, riboflavin, and magnesium. They are high in beneficial omega-3 fatty acids and vitamin E, an antioxidant that protects brain cells, promotes heart health, and lowers LDL (bad) cholesterol.

oats: Oat groats are whole grains that may be cut into pieces to make Scotch, steel-cut, or Irish oats, or steamed and rolled into old-fashioned, or rolled, oats. When the groats are cut into pieces and rolled thinner, they become quick-cooking oats. All of these forms retain their selenium and cholesterol-fighting nutrients, unlike instant oats. They are also high in vitamins B_1, B_6, and E.

onions: All onions contain organosulfur compounds that are thought to fight cancer and to promote heart health. Yellow and red onions also contain quercetin, which boosts these actions, while red onions have the added benefit of the antioxidant anthocyanin.

oranges: Famed for their high vitamin C content, oranges are also high in folate and potassium. They also provide limonoids and flavonoids, two disease-fighting antioxidants.

peaches: While its fuzzy skin is usually not eaten, the yellow or white flesh of the peach contains the vitamins A and C. Peaches are available either freestone or clingstone and can be found fresh, dried, frozen, and canned.

peanuts: Although they are not truly nuts, but legumes, peanuts are high in fat. They are a good source of protein, but they should be eaten in small amounts. Like most nuts, the fat they contain is largely monounsaturated.

pears: The beneficial pigments of pears are concentrated in their skin; as the skin is quite thin (except in the tan-skinned varieties), they can be eaten unpeeled, whether raw or cooked. The flesh contains vitamin A, as well as some phosphorus.

peas, English: Also called green, or garden, peas, they should be eaten soon after picking; they are also available frozen. They provide niacin and iron, along with vitamins A and C.

peas, split: When dried, the yellow or green field pea may be split at its natural seam for faster cooking in soups or purées. They are especially high in fiber and contain vitamin A.

peas, sugar snap: A cross between the English pea and the snow pea (mangetout), sugar snaps resemble the former but are entirely edible either cooked or raw. They provide vitmains A and C, along with folate, iron, phosphorus, and thiamin.

persimmons: Both the small, squat Fuyu, which is eaten when hard and crisp, and the larger, slightly pointed Hachiya, which is eaten when fully ripe, are rich in beta-carotenes and vitamin C.

pineapples: The pineapple's sweet, juicy flesh provides manganese, vitamins A and C, and bromelain, an antiflammatory enzyme that is also a digestive aid.

pine nuts: Delicate, buttery pine nuts contain both iron and thiamin. They are a favored garnish for salads and cooked foods.

plums: The edible skin of the plum, which comes in a variety of colors, contains most of its phytochemicals, although the yellow, purple, or red flesh also contains beneficial compounds. A good source of vitamin C, plums are one of the most healthful fruits. When they are not in season, enjoy them as prunes, their dried form.

polenta (corn): Although polenta may be made from other dried grains or white corn, usually it is coarsely or finely ground yellow cornmeal. Only stone-ground cornmeal is whole grain; store it in an airtight container in the refrigerator.

pomegranates: The fleshy seeds of this fruit are high in vitamin C, potassium, and heart-healthy anthocyanins. The fruit is in season during the fall months, while pomegranate juice is available year-round in natural foods stores and some other markets.

potatoes: The deeper the color of its pigment, the more healthful phytochemicals a potato possesses, but all potatoes are extremely rich in vitamins and minerals if eaten with the skin; they are also high in fiber. Make sure to buy organic potatoes; commercially grown potatoes contain high levels of pesticides.

prunes: These dried prune plums, now also called dried plums, are rich in vitamin A, potassium, and fiber. They are higher in antioxidants than any other fruit or vegetable, making them the top antiaging food.

pumpkins: The flesh of the pumpkin is nutrient rich with vitamin A and carotenoids, specifically the cancer-fighters alpha- and beta-carotene and lutein.

pumpkin seeds: High in fiber, protein, and various minerals, pumpkin seeds also contain beta-sisterol, which lowers cholesterol and

slows the growth of abnormal cells. Clean and toast your own, or buy them in natural foods stores or Latino markets.

quinoa: An ancient Incan grain, quinoa is higher in protein than all other grains, and its protein is complete. It is also rich in nutrients and unsaturated fat.

radicchio: A red-leafed member of the chicory family, radicchio comes in the loose-headed Verona variety and the tighter, more rounded Treviso variety. Both kinds have an assertive, bitter flavor, and both provide beneficial antioxidants such as anthocyanins and lycopene. Radicchio may be eaten raw, grilled, baked, or sautéed.

radishes: These peppery roots belong in the mustard family and are available in a variety of colors. They contain vitamin C and cancer-fighting antioxidants.

raisins: Antioxidant rich, raisins are also high in vitamins, minerals, and fiber. Both dark raisins and golden raisins (sultanas) start as green grapes, but golden raisins are treated with sulfur dioxide to prevent oxidation.

raspberries: Red raspberries have more fiber than most other fruits; they are also high in vitamin C and folate and extremely high in cancer-fighting antioxidants. Golden raspberries are less common, but they contain heart- and eye-healthy bioflavonoids. Although fresh raspberries are fragile, frozen unsweetened raspberries retain their flavor and are available year-round.

rhubarb: These tart red stalks are one of the first signs of spring when they appear in the market. High in vitamin A and beneficial phytochemicals, rhubarb helps protect the heart, boost immunity, and lower the risk of some cancers.

rice, brown: This whole grain retains its bran covering, making it high in fiber. Brown rice is available in long-, medium-, and short-

grain varieties. Like other whole grains, it is high in fiber and selenium; because the bran can become rancid at room temperature, brown rice it should be kept refrigerated.

rosemary: Used fresh or dried, this Mediterranean herb has a strong, fragrant flavor well suited to meats, poultry, seafood, and vegetables. It is a particularly good complement to roasted chicken and lamb.

rutabagas: Another member of the cabbage family, this yellow-skinned root vegetable has a mild-tasting yellow flesh. It contains vitamins A and C, as well as fiber and potassium.

sesame seeds: Flat and minute, sesame seeds come in several colors, but are most commonly a light ivory. They are rich in manganese, copper, and calcium, and also contain cholesterol-lowering lignans. Because they have a high oil content, they should be kept refrigerated. Toasting them briefly in a dry frying pan brings out their flavor.

shallots: Another onion family member, the shallot contains the same heart-healthy organosulfides as its relatives. It is milder in taste and more convenient to use in small amounts than the onion.

snow peas (mangetouts): Once both tips are pinched off, the thin, delicate snow pea is completely edible, either raw or cooked. It provides both calcium and iron.

spinach: High in a multitude of nutrients, from vitamins A, C, and K to folate and potassium, spinach is also one of the best sources of lutein, the carotenoid that prevents macular degeneration.

squash, summer: Most of the summer squash's nutrients are contained in its bright, edible yellow skin. It is a good source of manganese, as well as the carotenoids that give it its color.

squash, winter: The dense, meaty flesh of winter squashes is rich with vitamins A and C, folate, manganese, and potassium, as well as heart-protective and cancer-fighting carotenoids.

strawberries: Rich in antioxidant content, partly due to their anthocyanin pigments, strawberries are also extremely high in vitamin C. Because of these compounds, as well as their phenolic acids, these berries are thought to be important cancer-fighters.

sweet potatoes: The most commonly available of these root vegetables are a pale yellow variety and a dark orange one often erroneously referred to as a yam. Both are high in fiber, vitamins A and C, and a host of other vitamins and minerals, as well as more beta-carotene than any other vegetable.

Swiss chard: Yet another member of the far-flung cruciferous vegetable family, chard has dark green leaves and either white or red stalks and ribs. Along with cancer-fighting phytochemicals, it contains iron and vitamins A and C.

tomatillos: Sometimes called Mexican green tomatoes, tomatillos are firmer and less juicy than tomatoes and grow to ripeness inside a pale-green papery sheath. Used both raw and cooked, they are an essential sweet-sour ingredient in many Mexican green sauces. Look for fresh or canned tomatillos in well-stocked supermarkets or Latin groceries.

tomatoes: Not only are tomatoes high in vitamin C, they are also high in fiber and have good amounts of other vitamins and minerals. Tomatoes also contain lycopene, which lowers cancer risk. The body absorbs this antioxidant better when tomatoes are cooked, making tomato sauce and tomato paste especially healthful.

vinegar: Many types are available, made from a variety of red or white wines or, like cider vinegar and rice vinegar, from fruits

and grains. Vinegars are further seasoned by infusing them with fresh herbs, fruit, garlic, or other flavorful ingredients. All offer a healthful, low-fat way to season a range of foods.

watercress: This spicy green is, surprisingly, a cruciferous vegetable. It contains good amounts of vitamins A and C. The peppery taste of watercress is due to a certain isothiocyanate that has shown the potential to help combat lung cancer.

watermelon: Despite its high water content, this melon provides vitamins A and C, along with the anthocyanins that give it its color.

wheat, whole (wholemeal): The bran in whole wheat contains selenium and other minerals, as well as vitamin E. Whole wheat is also an important source of fiber, which is thought to help lower the risk of strokes and heart disease. As with all whole grains, all forms of whole wheat, from wheat germ to flour, should be kept refrigerated.

wine: The colors of red and rosé wines are due to the skins of the purple grapes used to make the wines; red wine has more beneficial flavonoids than grape juice. These phytochemicals have been shown to help increase "good" HDL cholesterol.

yogurt: The bacterial cultures in yogurt are prized as an aid in digestion. Like the milk it is made from, yogurt can be full fat, low fat, or nonfat.

zucchini (courgettes): Most of the zucchini's nutrients are found in its skin, which contains phytochemicals that strengthen the eyes, bones, and teeth; help to boost immunity; and lower the risk of some cancers.

Bibliography

The resources below were used in the creation of this book, and are recommended for further reading on the subject of colorful plant foods:

BOOKS

Gollman, Barbara, and Kim Pierce. *The Phytopia Cookbook*. Dallas, Tex.: Phytopia, Inc., 1998.

Green, Eliza. *Field Guide to Produce*. Philadephia: Quirk Books, 2004.

Heber, David, M.D., Ph.D. *What Color Is Your Diet?* New York: Harper Collins, 2001.

Hess, Mary Abbott, L.H.D., M.S., R.D., F.A.D.A; Dana Jacobi; and Marie Simmons. *Williams-Sonoma Essentials of Healthful Cooking*. Menlo Park, Calif.: Oxmoor House, 2003.

Joseph, James A., Ph.D.; Daniel A. Nadeau, M.D.; and Anne Underwood. *The Color Code*. New York: Hyperion, 2002.

Pivonka, Elizabeth, R.D., Ph.D., and Barbara Berry, M.S., R.D. *5 a Day: The Better Health Cookbook*. New York: Rodale, 2002.

Tantillo, Tony, and Sam Gugino. *Eat Fresh, Stay Healthy*. New York: Macmillan General Reference, 1997.

WEBSITES

Centers for Disease Control:
http://www.cdc.gov

National Cancer Institute:
http://www.nci.nih.gov

Produce for Better Health Foundation:
http://www.5aday.org

United States Department of Agriculture:
http://www.usda.gov

University of California, Berkeley, School of Public Health Wellness Letter:
http://www.wellnessletter.com

Index

FREE PRESS

A Division of Simon & Schuster, Inc.
1230 Avenue of the Americas
New York, NY 10020

WILLIAMS-SONOMA

Founder & Vice-Chairman Chuck Williams

WELDON OWEN INC.

Chief Executive Officer John Owen
President and Chief Operating Officer Terry Newell
Chief Financial Officer Christine E. Munson
Vice President International Sales Stuart Laurence
Creative Director Gaye Allen
Publisher Hannah Rahill
Associate Publisher Sarah Putman Clegg
Editor Emily Miller
Editorial Assistant Juli Vendzules
Photo Director and Senior Designer Marisa Kwek
Production Director Chris Hemesath
Color Manager Teri Bell
Production and Reprint Coordinator Todd Rechner

THE WILLIAMS-SONOMA NEW HEALTHY KITCHEN *MAIN DISHES*

Conceived and produced by Weldon Owen Inc.
814 Montgomery Street, San Francisco, CA 94133
Telephone: 415 291 0100   Fax: 415 291 8841

In collaboration with Williams-Sonoma, Inc.
3250 Van Ness Avenue, San Francisco, CA 94109

A WELDON OWEN PRODUCTION
Copyright © 2006 by Weldon Owen Inc. and Williams-Sonoma Inc.

For information regarding special discounts for bulk purchases, please contact Simon & Schuster Special Sales at 1-800-456-6798 or business@simonandschuster.com

Set in Vectora

Color separations by Mission Productions Limited.
Printed and bound in Hong Kong by Midas Printing.

First printed in 2005.

10 9 8 7 6 5 4 3 2 1

Library of Congress Cataloging-in-Publication data is available.

ISBN-13: 978-0-7432-7859-1
ISBN-10: 0-7432-7859-3

ACKNOWLEDGMENTS

Weldon Owen wishes to thank the following people for their generous support in producing this book:
Copy Editor Carolyn Miller; Consulting Editor Judith Dunham; Proofreaders Desne Ahlers and Carrie Bradley; Indexer Ken DellaPenta;
Adrienne Aquino; Shadin Saah; Carol Hacker; Jackie Mills; Marianne Mitten; and Richard Yu.

Photographer Dan Goldberg

Photographer's Assistant Julie Caine

Food Stylist Jen Straus

Assistant Food Stylist Max La Rivière-Hedrick

Photographer Ben Dearnley

Food and Prop Stylist Julz Beresford

Assistant Food Stylist Jess Sly

The images on the following pages were created by this photo team:
8–9; 18 *top left;* 31; 32; 34 *bottom left, bottom right;* 37, 44; 45 *bottom;* 47; 48; 51; 52 *top left, bottom right;* 55; 56; 59; 62 *top;* 63 *bottom;* 69; 70 *top left;* 73; 77; 80 *top;* 81 *top;* 84; 88; 90 *bottom left, bottom right;* 93; 100 *top;* 101 *bottom;* 108 *top right;* 119 *bottom.*

The images on the following pages were created by this photo team:
18 *top right, bottom left, bottom right;* 21; 22; 25; 26; 28; 29; 34 *top left, top right;* 38; 41; 42; 45 *top;* 52 *top right, bottom left;* 60; 62 *bottom;* 63 *top;* 65; 66; 70 *top right, bottom left, bottom right;* 74; 78; 80 *bottom;* 81 *bottom;* 83; 87; 88; 90 *top left, top right;* 94; 97; 98; 100 *bottom;* 101 *top;* 102; 104; 107; 108 *top left, bottom left, bottom right;* 112; 115; 116; 118; 119 *top;* 121; 122; 125.

A NOTE ON WEIGHTS AND MEASURES

All recipes include customary U.S. and metric measurements. Metric conversions are based on a standard developed for these books and have been rounded off. Actual weights may vary.